ECOPHILOSOPHY
A Field Guide to the Literature

Donald Edward Davis

R. & E. Miles

*San Pedro * 1989*

Cover designed by Kim Tibballs

Textual type set by Kirk B. Smith, LP (Brooklyn, NY)
Cover, display type set by Entropy Enterprises (San Pedro, CA)
Printed on acid-free paper and bound by Thompson-Shore (Dexter, MI)

Peace and Plenty

R. & E. Miles
Post Office Box 1916
San Pedro, California 90733
(213) 833-8856

Naturam expellas furca, temen usque recurrent.

Horace
Epistles, I. x.24.

CONTENTS

FOREWORD

Many years ago, while on the faculty of a small eastern Washington college, I was asked to take part in a panel discussion of Rachel Carson's just-published *Silent Spring*. The college was in an agricultural community, and two of the faculty panelists were also farmers. One of them was a soils expert who had recently moved to the area. The other was a historian who was born on a fruit ranch in the valley. The discussion that evening was soon polarized between those whose personal experience inclined them toward thinking ecologically, and those who were used to thinking within narrowly defined disciplines. The entomologist on the panel thought that Carson's book was exaggerated, an over-reaction. The agricultural technician dismissed the book as propaganda for "bird watchers and Nature lovers." The historian was inclined to agree with Carson, for he had a broad perspective based on personal experience in farming for three generations in the valley. His family had been making note of the changes in insect populations over the years.

During the course of the evening, the word "ecology" came up only a few times, but it was clear that some of the participants were thinking systemically about our practices, and some were not. Those who were thinking systemically sided with Carson. This discussion took place in the early 1960s. Little did we then suspect that we were at the beginning of a complex and turbulent period of social and cultural change in which the environmental elements would play a major part.

Looking back, it seems plain that what began in the 1960s with the publication of Carson's book was destined to reach the 1980s as a broad, multi-dimensional, cross-disciplinary critique of Western industrial society. Moreover, it involved not only critique, but a healing movement toward creation of a new culture of wholeness and harmony with Nature. This same creative energy is revitalizing many of the ecologically sound elements of our cultural heritage. It has given new life to everything from philosophy and theology to hiking and gardening. What emerged during this process of analysis, exploration, and practice is what is now called *ecophilosophy*. As Donald Edward Davis has emphasized here and elsewhere, a philosophy which is ecological in the fullest sense will require the coming together of diverse human endeavors in both their theoretical and practical forms. In his view, ecophilosophy represents a holistic coming together of environment, activity, and idea; a way of thinking that will concretely illuminate humankind's rightful place in the natural world.

As many of the texts cited in this bibliography illustrate, modern industrial culture has been marked by continuous movement into fragmentation of the object side of life, and alienation from the subject side—which is the natural ground of human Being in the world. The views of knowledge which emerged in modern philosophy pulled Western character and culture loose from their moorings.

Ecophilosophy emerged during the past 30 years as a response to this condition of fragmentation and drift, but even more importantly it emerged as a result of a concern for more than human self-interest. Environmentalism as a political phenomenon was first motivated by concern for human welfare. But people who became involved in environmental activism soon broadened their concerns. To broaden one's concerns beyond ego and then beyond human species is a necessary development in the process of human maturation to planetary responsibility; that is, for assuming responsibility to live in a way that is light on oneself, others and the Earth.

It is true that before Carson's book there was conservation and preservation environmental politics. People like John Muir, Aldo Leopold, and Gifford Pinchot and organizations like the Sierra Club and the Wilderness Society come to mind. However, when Carson's book was published, such organizations were mainly focused on preserving and saving wilderness areas and conserving wildlife. Environmental politics was fairly confined. Activists wrote letters to legislators and executives; they went to hearings on park proposals; and they tried to rally short-term support to pass specific proposals. The environmental movement, as a broad-based social movement, began to emerge only in the early 60s.

More than any other book, Carson's *Silent Spring* presented some of the basic concepts of ecology in a way that made perfect sense—at least to many people who had already been active in "conservation" organizations, for their own experiences in Nature gave them insight into ecological processes. Environmental impact statements, the National Environmental Policy Act, and a host of other acts and agencies, were not as yet conceived. Nonetheless, it is clear that some persons had already made or begun the journey to a deeper ecological consciousness, one that transcended the ways of thought characteristic of most conservation organizations thirty years ago. What explains their relatively minor influence, until after the 60s, is in part the visibility of environmental degradation, which on a large scale became obvious to many only after the 60s. Moreover, the threats to the integrity of the environment that people like Leopold and Muir reacted to were minor compared to those that emerged in the 60s. This was because the level of technological power, although great then, was modest compared to what emerged in the 50s and 60s. The technologies of war now have global effects and could bring about the death of Nature. The introduction of persistent, human-made chemicals that are capable of moving through whole ecosystems has become commonplace. The negative effects of industrial technology on the environment became intensified and undeniable.

Carson's sensibilities, her talents as an author, and her training as an ocean scientist, enabled her to convey a holistic understanding of human effects on the Natural world. Through her eyes we were able to see the reasons for the futile cycle of accelerating pesticide use and increasing problems with "pests" and other negative consequences. She enabled us to see the potential and real effects our agricultural technologies could have on ourselves. Once this holistic way of thinking and perceiving began to be discussed, it was seen to tie in directly to the experiential dimensions of wilderness experience, gardening, and naturalistic art. The confluence of field ecology, wilderness experience, ecopolitics and philosophy of Nature was to lead to a renewal of insight and understanding of Nature religions and primal ways of life; it was also to stimulate new appreciation for the inspirational and spiritual aspects of art (in the broad sense) and the Natural world.

In looking back over the past thirty years, many trends stand out as important, but one of the most significant was the change in consciousness and culture that the development of ecophilosophy involved. In many respects, we could say that the meeting place for all of the divergent ways of protecting the Natural world, appreciating other life forms, celebrating embodied planetary life, reclaiming our ancient roots, realizing ourselves as part of the larger living world of Nature, developing a sense of the Cosmos, all of these come together in ecophilosophy. If we ask what ecophilosophy is, we can say it is the development of a truly ecological philosophy and sensibility. There is no way that this can be accomplished without far-ranging questioning and exploration that takes one through all of these and other areas.

The neologism "ecophilosophy" came into use, then, during a period when environmental degradation was reaching global proportions with accelerating species extinction, alteration of weather patterns, thinning of the ozone shield, death of forests from acid rain, and so on. It came into prominence during a time when several different disciplines were paving the way for a new ontology a new epistemology and a new cosmology. This new worldview has many affinities with the perennial wisdom of divergent traditions, especially in the domain of ecowisdom, or Earthwisdom.

At first, during the late 60s and early 70s, philosophers and other scholars started developing what they called environmental philosophy. Many of them were preoccupied with the construction of an environmental ethic, which would be an analytical extension of current ethical theories. In this approach, preservation of the environment could be seen to arise as a natural corollary of human ethics, for if persons have inherent worth, and they depend on the environment, then our treatment of the environment has ethical implications—just so far as it affects actual or potential human persons. These were primarily axiological approaches, which attempted to identify a limited number of fundamental principles, and from these deduce and develop a comprehensive environmental ethic. As time went on, it became clear that an environmental ethic by itself was not going to go deep enough to appreciate the nature of the problems facing us. As Wendell Berry observed, environmental crises are crises of both character and culture.

Reform environmentalism (as it came to be called), as a political response to environmental degradation, was piecemeal and issue oriented, and it fit well with the environmental ethics approach. It, too, did not look deep enough into the source of our values, but tried only to ameliorate our effects. It philosophized and politicked without questioning the assumptions of the acquisitive, consumption-oriented society. Narrowly conceived environmental ethics, too, was only reformist; it did not involve moving to an ecological consciousness. Dissatisfied, some philosophers looked for a more comprehensive approach.

Out of this ferment there emerged a more radical critique of the philosophical foundations of Western industrial society. Persons engaged in environmental philosophy came to see that developing environmental ethics as a practical way, cannot proceed so long as one merely extends ethical systems that are based on anthropocentrism and not on an ecological philosophy. Environmental studies and problems are by their very nature transdisciplinary, and many of those involved in environmental philosophy soon realized that progress required a much broader context of knowledge than that provided by reformist ethics. Thus "environmental philosophy" came to stand for a more expansive approach to the philosophy of Nature. Environmental philosophers sought to articulate an environmental ethic dependent on an ecological worldview. This meant for them that we have to understand the nature of the problems in terms of the interrelationships between our desires, concepts, beliefs, characters and cultures, and how these produce technology practices and lifestyles that affect on the Natural world in various ways.

The first phase of the deeper philosophical undertaking was aimed at understanding ecologically (in the broad sense) the condition we are in, but the next phase involved an attempt to go beyond critique to the development of new visions, new ecologically informed ways of understanding and living. When these all flow together, the quest is for what Arne Naess calls ecosophy, or ecological wisdom, which is both a practical way of life and realization of the highest states of being with intrinsic worth. Sometime during this process, "ecophilosophy" replaced "environmental philosophy" as the generic term by means of which to characterize this deeper turn toward Nature. From the current vantage point, then, ecophilosophy can be seen as connected with very ancient Socratic traditions in Western philosophy, the pursuit of self-knowledge and realization, but it also reaches back to the Nature connection found in the earliest forms of Pythagoreanism and their Orphic backgrounds, as well as to the Old Ways of hunter-gatherers, such as the Native Americans. Ecophilosophy also involves elements from the current scientific and technological contexts.

In its literal sense, "ecophilosophy" means the love of wisdom of household place, or less literally, the loving pursuit and realization of the wisdom of dwelling in harmony with one's place. The animating spirit of ecophilosophy is evident in its urge to understand the human condition, the nature of the human self with its ecology, and the place of human Being in Nature's scheme; but it also aspires to see Nature as it is in itself, not as It is imagined to be, and to relate to the Natural world not just intellectually but with one's whole being.

Engaging in ecophilosophy is both inquiry and practice. Its pursuit helps us to appreciate and understand our embodied life on Earth, in our particular culture, time and place, as a particular species among others. How does our culture help or hinder us in the achievement of ecological harmony and peace? What ecophilosophical practice will best help us to achieve ecosophy, that is, ecological wisdom—as dwelling harmoniously in a place?

We can see from what has been said that ecophilosophy is not just an academic game played with symbols and words. As we noted above, in its roots ecophilosophy signifies the love and pursuit of the wisdom dwelling in place, so as to dwell wisely within it. Wisdom unifies practice, knowledge and experience in action appropriate to place. "Place" here refers not just to physical location, but to our whole household, with all of its many living communities, our place in the scheme of things.

There are several species of ecophilosophy now in evidence in the literature. Some ecophilosophies are tacit, created and developed over a long time, while others are a product of explicit, conscious design. All involve both tacit and explicit ecological elements and understanding. All are in part intuitive, in part experimental, in part reflective, and in part aesthetic. Some examples of ecophilosophies include the social and religious practices of the Maring, the ecological Hinduism of the Bishnois, the rituals and renewal festivals of Nature-awe religions, the Taoism of Lao-Tzu, Arne Naess's *Ecosophy-T*, George Sessions' and Bill Devall's *Deep Ecology*, Henryk Skolimowski's *Design-Tactics-Ecophilosophy*, and Murray Bookchin's *Social Ecology*. In our current context, we are faced with a severe disharmony between human activities and the long-term sustainable integrity of biological communities. This is part of the reason for the emergence of a conscious effort to design an applied ecophilosophy.

In an approach that celebrates diversity, there is not one and only one sound ecophilosophy, in terms of specific details, since the relevant context determines the appropriateness of a particular ecophilosophy. The Earth has diverse places, and each has its ways to be respected. Moreover, it makes more sense from the standpoint of human health, development, interest, and survival to have a diversity of cultures that are each practicing ecologically sound ways of life. Nonetheless, a full appreciation for the concept of ecophilosophy leads us to say that all deep ecophilosophies will be paths which have a core of ecosophy, and this ecosophy will have common elements.

The depth of an ecophilosophy, then, is measured in part by its capacity to create practices, traditions, cultures and characters which are able not merely to exist, but to dwell and *flourish* on this Earth, in a particular bioregion and specific place, in a way that is sustainable, tolerant and accepting of other cultures, characters, practices and life forms. It increases the possibility for persons to realize ecological wisdom. Authentic ecophilosophical depth begins when we not merely affirm the intrinsic value of other beings, but also when we genuinely achieve intimate reciprocal relationships with them—through forms of life which enable us to have an extended and deep sense of identification with them. Ecosophy, then, is not sentimentality, but involves a deep love for the Earth and its beings. To study nature objectively, as object or thing, produces a certain limited but useful knowledge; however, to understand it more fully as a whole requires deep sensibilities, and this receptive relationship is also necessary if we are to fully realize our own greatest potentials. The movement to ecosophy is nothing less than a movement from self-centeredness to reality centeredness, and the latter is neither objectless-subjectivity, nor subjectless-objectivity, but integrated-wholeness.

As noted in this volume's introduction, ecophilosophies are expressed in styles of life that yield particular kinds of wisdom and understanding. As it has emerged, ecophilosophy is not just a theory, but a way of living, about which we can theorize, which we can celebrate in story, poem or song, or realize in our daily practices.

By this circuitous route we come at last to Donald Davis' book, *Ecophilosophy: A Field Guide to the Literature*. Its value and importance should be clear from what has been said. The growth of the literature in ecophilosophy over the past 25 years has been prodigious. A person approaching this area for the first time hardly knows where to start. Even someone who has worked in this area throughout this period could have missed something of importance. The time is ripe, then, for the appearance of such an annotated bibliography.

The field guide Davis offers aims to fill this need. It is well done in selection and annotation, given the limits and biases to which he confesses in his Introduction. As such works go, this one has been carried out with care. It reads with exceptional clarity and will be a valuable aid, both to beginners and to those who have labored long in these areas.

Ecophilosophy, as represented here, is one of the most important and central undertakings of our time. It cuts across ideological, national, and discipline boundaries. It is indispensable to the creation of new technology practices and cultural forms that are not merely ecologically harmonious but enriching and ennobling. Davis' bibliography will make this undertaking more accessible for the participation of a wider public. It should help to facilitate the meeting and joining of our collective efforts toward addressing human and environmental problems. Nothing is more urgent than to find a common ground where all people can work together for the life of the planet. Ecophilosophical practices appreciative of planet Earth are such a common ground.

Alan R. Drengson
University of Victoria, 1988

PREFACE

The following bibliography represents a compilation of texts directly or indirectly related to the school of thought commonly referred to as ecophilosophy. It is designed as both reference tool and educative guidebook and can be used by the newcomer to the field or the specialist.

Limitations of space did not allow for lengthy analysis of any of the works cited. Recognizable benchmarks in the field were, however, given considerable space and attention. In all applicable cases I have chosen to include subtitles, which should help the reader better locate a work within a particular discipline. All titles appear numerically, alphabetically by author(s) or editor(s), and are entered according to standard bibliographic citation. The book's index, which refers to entry numbers only, provides additional access to the authors, other individuals, and all other major subject areas appearing in the field guide. Despite the fact that many of the volumes are out-of-print in their original form, first edition sources were cited as often as possible. Occasionally, when exceptional reprints were known to me (such as Peregrine Smith's reprint of John Muir's *Wilderness Essays*), the more recent edition was chosen.

The author apologizes in advance for omissions. Completeness in a bibliography such as this is regrettably unattainable. Appendixes have been included in order to assist the reader in locating materials not included under this cover. To eliminate omissions created by the temporal restraints of the publishing industry, forthcoming texts have also been included.

ACKNOWLEDGEMENTS

To undertake a project of this magnitude, one must spend many solitary hours sifting and sorting through mounds of resource materials. The final result, however, was hardly a solitary effort—many have contributed to this ecophilosophical field guide. I would like to especially thank Daniel Chodorkoff, John Clark, and Andrew Kimbrell for their many helpful suggestions related to a number of the annotated entries. For general support and professional advisement over the past several years, I would also like to thank Lewis Sumberg, Ralph Hood, Jr., Michael Edmondson, Murray Bookchin, Jeremy Rifkin, Nicanor Perlas, Alan Drengson, Glenn McRae, and Marc LaFountain. Many thanks also go to Kimberly Tibbals for putting up with my long "leaves-of-absence" and cross-country research stints. Lastly, I would like to acknowledge the heroic efforts of Kirk B. Smith; as well as thank the many unnamed individuals who have assisted me at the following libraries: The Irvine Sullivan Ingram Library, West Georgia College; The Lupton Library, The University of Tennessee at Chattanooga; The Bicentennial Library, Chattanooga, Tennessee; The Library of Congress, Washington, D.C., and Emory University's Robert W. Woodruff Library in Atlanta, Georgia.

INTRODUCTION

The environmental turn in philosophical literature has created a renaissance in the study of humankind and nature. Philosophy has indeed "gone wild."[1] In most popular and academic circles this rapidly growing literature is commonly referred to as deep ecology, ecosophy, environmental philosophy, philosophical ecology, or simply, ecophilosophy. While the former labels seem to have direct associations with individual thinkers or particular trains of thought, ecophilosophy, a much broader, more generic term, remains on the whole disassociated from any foundational presuppositions or exclusionary philosophical systems. Because this literature review similarly reflects the diversity of a discipline unbound by central messages or single, one-dimensional visions, the title *Ecophilosophy: A Field Guide to the Literature* was chosen.

As its fundamental tenet, ecophilosophy seeks the unqualified re-unification of humans with nature; a moral and political order where human civilization is brought into harmony with the natural world. In achieving this goal, ecophilosophy has acquired no single method of inquiry; it has been significantly influenced by a number of areas of study. In varying degrees, ecophilosophy has borrowed from environmental ethics, human ecology, natural science, humanistic geography, social ecology, natural history, cultural anthropology, analytic philosophy, ecological feminism, animal rights theory, environmental psychology, theology and religion, environmental history, existentialism, Marxism, the philosophy of technology, Green politics, and scientific ecology. While at first glance it would appear that ecophilosophy might suffer from an acute eclecticism, it has, of late, been able to maintain a relatively autonomous identity. Ecophilosophy, it seems, is more than the sum of its interdisciplinary parts.

A comprehensive guide to (or study of) ecophilosophy should do more than simply illustrate its diverse character, however. Many ecophilosophers are adding an intellectual depth and unity to the study of both humans and nature, influencing not only the academy, but creating important ethical guides for social and human conduct as well. The enormous popularity of Devall and Sessions' *Deep Ecology*, Morris Berman's *The Reenchantment of the World*, and Fritjof Capra's *The Turning Point* illustrates the potential translation of ecophilosophical principles to public policy and to the society at large. At the same time, the intellectual and

---

1. See, for example, Holmes Rolston, III, *Philosophy Gone Wild* (Buffalo, New York: Prometheus Books, 1986).

philosophical rigor of the writings of Erazim Kohák, Murray Bookchin, Neil Evernden, Hans Jonas, and Arne Naess points to philosophies of nature capable of withstanding the slings and arrows of even the most critical metalinguistic theories of postmodern philosophical debate.

Despite its recognized virtues, ecophilosophy is certainly not without its theoretical problems, nor immune to the conceptual pitfalls of traditional analytic philosophy. Since ecophilosophy is concerned not only with sustaining lifestyles that celebrate nature's rich diversity, but also interested in formulating a coherent body of ideas, the possibility of cultivating this ecological sensibility, a *living* philosophy, remains to a large extent, problematic. Nature philosophers have for the most part always reduced nature to *theoria*, or reified theories about nature.[2] And those philosophers who have taken our experience of nature seriously have just as often subjected this experience to a mythical or mystical "oneness"—or what G. W. F. Hegel called in *The Phenomenology of Spirit*, "a night in which all cows are black." The task of critically articulating our experience of nature, without over-conceptualizing it—so that our reflections of nature give credence to both thinking and living ecologically—seems to be the most important assignment for future ecophilosophical pursuits.

The practical question of how a larger public might acquire (or recapture) the sensibilities currently embraced by ecophilosophy is an important one. In his book *The PostModern Condition*, Jean-Francois Lyotard has provocatively reported on the cultural acquisition of knowledge in highly technologized cultures like our own. Lyotard argues that social and political realities in postindustrial society are not maintained by any inherent or substantive truths; they are controlled *information-ally*, that is, by the most prevailing or dominant discourse or "narratives." Whether or not one agrees with Lyotard's fundamental thesis, the problem of language reification, and the social legitimation of such information is, as Lyotard suggests, a crucial existential problem in today's fragmented society.[3] The narratives of ecophilosophy, without an ecological practice or history to inform them, will do very little to transform philosophical ecology into a living tradition of ideas; a body of knowledge embodied.

As one might expect, most of the discussions surrounding the more metaphysical assumptions of ecophilosophy revolve around less explicit ecological concerns. At its most theoretical level, ecophilosophy remains preoccupied with conceptual

---

2. R. G. Collingwood's classic study, *The Ideal of Nature*, is a case in point. See also Erazim Kohák's discussion of this philosophical caveat in *The Embers and the Stars* (Chicago: University of Chicago Press, 1984), pp. 180–82.

3. Jean-Francois Lyotard, *The PostModern Condition* (Minneapolis: University of Minnesota Press, 1984). For a less "text-centric" discussion on the segmentation of modern consciousness, one that stresses the psychic cohesiveness of community and ecological reconstruction, see Yi-Fu Tuan, *Segmented Worlds and Self* (Minneapolis: University of Minnesota Press, 1982).

issues like "intrinsic value" and the "ontology of self." Interestingly, these conceptual issues have created the most fundamental divisions among the theories of ecophilosophy's leading practitioners.[4]

Ecophilosophy's most polemical discussions are, in fact, those which appear along the axes of what I call the homocentric/biocentric, human/nonhuman doublets. While biocentric philosophers like Paul Taylor, Warwick Fox, Arne Naess, and others have argued passionately for a nonanthropocentric ecological ethic, their critics have argued (for various reasons) that biocentrism uncritically removes humanity from a dominant position in the natural order.[5] In essence, the biocentric position argues that just as the Copernican revolution removed the earth from the center of the universe, the ecological revolution removes man from the center of the earth or biosphier "the measure of all things," but an active participant in a vast organic universe. Since all life-forms interact equally with one another in the biocentric view, "respect for nature" becomes as much (if not more) a moral imperative as our conventional "respect for persons." Thus, the biocentric philosophers maintain that any attempt to erect an ecological ethics that is primarily concerned with human-centered interests will, ecologically speaking, fail.

On the more homocentric side of the discussion, critics of the biocentric world view like Henryk Skolimowski, Richard Watson, and Patrick Dooley have argued that biocentrism's radical egalitarianism makes humans, in the words of Christian theologian Francis Schaeffer, "no more than the grass."[6] The homocentric advocates argue that biocentrism converts the inherent value of all living things into an *equal* ranking: the lives of humans become no more or less respected than the lives of wild flowers, insects, trees, or whales. Although some biocentric philosophers like Arne Naess and Paul Taylor have recently revised their positions to accommodate these criticisms, the debate surrounding the human/nonhuman aspects of ecological axiology will undoubtedly continue.[7] This bibliography pays considerable attention to this issue: relevant commentaries reflect an intentional preoccupation with the human/non-human debate previously outlined.

As the lines for and against a human-centered environmental ethics were being drawn in the 1970s, in journals like Environmental Ethics and Environmental Review, the ecophilosophical corpus saw in the 1980s the introduction of more phenomenologically grounded interpretations of the nature/human relationship. Michael Zimmerman, Erazim Kohák, Neil Evernden, Joseph Grange, Bruce Foltz,

---

4. An execellent summary of these divisions and philosophical differences can be found in the Fall 1986 issue of *The Trumpeter* (the journal of the Canadian Ecophilosophy Network), Vol. 3, No. 4. See particularly the discussion by Skolimowski, Naess, Devall, and Fox.

5. Ecophilosophers have also suggested that *all* ecological ethics, biocentric or otherwise, are perhaps only remodeled traditional humanistic ethics. See, for example, Holmes Rolston, III, "Is There An Ecological Ethic?," *Ethics* 85 (1975), pp. 93–109; see also Patrick K. Dooley, "The Ambiguity of Environmental Ethics: Duty or Heroism?," *Philosophy Today* 31 (Spring 1986), pp. 48–57.

and David Seamon have all made important contributions to this end. In many ways their writings have steered clear of the normative metaphysics so characteristic of the earlier ecophilosophical literature. Indeed, the best of these studies have provided readers with nature ontologies that are both philosophically sophisticated and empirically sound. Unfortunately, a great deal of this literature is still burdened by the political quietism pervading phenomenological discourse in general.

Thus far, I have introduced ecophilosophy in mostly philosophical terms. But as noted in the preface, one does not have to be a philosopher, in the purely academic sense, to be an *eco*philosopher. Appreciation for nature extends beyond all economic, social, religious, political, and philosophical boundaries. Ecophilosophy is not just about self-reflexive introspection, but about personal, social, and political empowerment as well. Whereas present philosophy is unapologetically analytic, language oriented, environmentally and ecologically oblivious, ecophilosophy is "comprehensive, spiritually alive, pursuing wisdom, life-oriented, environmentally and ecologically conscious, socially concerned. . . ."[8] Writes Alan Drengson of the University of Victoria in British Columbia:

Ecophilosophy is measured in part by its capacity to create practices, traditions, cultures, and characters which are able not merely to exist but to dwell and flourish on Earth. . . . Ecophilosophies, as inquiries and activities of a certain form, are expressed in styles of life that yield particular kinds of wisdom and understandingecophilosophy is not just a theory, but a way of living. . . .[9]

As an *applied* discipline, ecophilosophy may make transparent the conditions of its own theoretical possibilities by questioning the level at which theory informs, or is informed by, ecological practices. This application of theoretical concepts to practical concerns, though essential to ecophilosophy, should be a criterion for all philosophical pursuits. Henry David Thoreau, himself an avowed pragmatist, saw the philosopher's role as guided by such practical utilitarian concerns. "To be a philosopher," he argued in *Walden*, "is not merely to found a school, but to love wisdom according to its dictates, a life of simplicity, independence, magnanimity, and trust. It is to solve some of the problems of life, not only theoretically, but practically."[10]

As we approach the next millennium of human history, we need to begin seriously thinking about how we might incorporate the ecophilosophical attitude into a

---

6. Francis Schaeffer, *Pollution and the Death of Man: The Christian View of Ecology* (Wheaton, IL: Tyndale House Publishers, 1970), pp. 17–33.

7. See Arne Naess, "Deep Ecology in Good Conceptual Health," *The Trumpeter* 3 (Fall, 1986), pp. 1821; Paul Taylor, *Respect for Nature: A Theory of Environmental Ethics*.

8. George Sessions, Review of Henryk Skolimowski's *Ecophilosophy: Designing New Tactics for Living, Environmental Ethics* 6 (Summer, 1984), p. 169.

9. Alan Drengson, "Editor's Introduction," *The Trumpeter* 3 (Fall, 1986), pp. 1–2.

responsible political platform applicable to all realms of personal and social experience. Considering the severity of the present ecological crisis, it is equally important that ecophilosophy discuss how already existing ecological existences can be preserved from the secular knife of an increasingly totalitarian technology. Having grown up in the shadows of the southern Appalachian foothills, I have personally witnessed an entire way of life, an ecological *culture*, destroyed by the effects of ecological carelessness, human greed, and corporate imperialism. Without political and personal empowerment, no culture can withstand the onslaughts of the runaway industrial machine. Ecophilosophy must be able to effectively articulate a viable philosophy of sustainable right praxis, a "practice guided by theory in its broadest and deepest sense."[11]

In the following pages I have assembled and commented on a variety of ecophilosophical and related texts. While many of the volumes argue for a "right ecological philosophy," others offer only a parochial version of it. In the written exposition, ecological or otherwise, there is always the danger of philosophical abstraction, which will please the intellectual vanguard, but will have insignificant effect on the lived world of everyday experience. Scholasticism of this kind has an appropriate and important place in the ecophilosophical project, but ecophilosophy is (or should be) much more than this. As noted earlier, ecophilosophy is also the creation of a new political awareness; philosophies of practice capable of sustaining ecological lifestyles while at the same time meeting and offering alternative solutions to the problems of contemporary life.[12]

Without question, many of the authors represented in this bibliography would deny any professional or personal relationship to something called "ecophilosophy." Nonetheless, may I remind the reader here, in closing, that this bibliography's *raison d'être* was not simply to assemble texts that were, per se, ecophilosophical. My goal was to compile and comment on a body of knowledge that has been, or could been used to provide a better understanding of humanity's place in the natural world. Ecophilosophy should appeal to a variety of people on a variety of levels; I sincerely hope that this bibliography, this ecophilosophical field guide, will be helpful to that end.

Donald Edward Davis
Washington, D.C., 1988

---

10. Henry David Thoreau, *The Writings of Henry David Thoreau*, Bradford Torrey, Ed., (Boston, Houghton Mifflin Company, 1906), Volume II, p. 16.

11. Murray Bookchin, "Toward a Philosophy of Nature—The Bases for an Ecological Ethics," Michael Tobias, Ed., *Deep Ecology* (San Diego: Avant Books, 1985), p. 215.

12. How philosophy might critically provide such ecological solutions, so that "its project can concentrate on the preservation and expansion of wilderness," is addressed in Christopher Manes, "Philosophy and the Environmental Task," *Environmental Ethics* 10 (Spring, 1988), pp. 75–82.

In the relations of man with the animals, with the flowers, with the objects of creation, there is a great ethic, scarcely perceived as yet, which will at length break forth into the light and which will be the corollary and complement to human ethics.

Victor Hugo

THE FIELD GUIDE

1. **Abbey, Edward. The Monkey Wrench Gang.**
Salt Lake City, UT: Dream Garden Press, 1985
(Tenth Anniversary Edition). 356 pages.

A tale of four defenders of the canyon country of the American Southwest, *The Monkey Wrench Gang* has inspired an entirely new breed of outlaw environmentalists—*monkey wrenchers.* Modern day monkey wrenchers, like the characters in Abbey's controversial novel, go about the countryside wreaking havoc (ecotage) on corporate and State development. Although the practice of monkey-wrenching has certainly never been officially "endorsed" by ecophilosophers, it has nevertheless become a common practice of members of such environmental groups as *Earth First!* While some practitioners of monkey-wrenching have been rightly criticized as being "anti-humanists" or even "terrorists," Abbey makes a strong case for the practice, arguing that anti-development ecotage is, in some highly qualified cases, morally justifiable.

2. **Abbey, Edward. One Life at a Time, Please.**
New York, NY: Henry Holt, 1988. 225 pages.

A diverse collection of previously published essays by one of the most controversial figures in environmental literature. One finds an interview with Joseph Wood Krutch, an essay about San Francisco, a diatribe against cowboys, a study of Ralph Waldo Emerson, and a television script written for an NBC television show entitled *Almanac.* Abbey's work evokes strong negative reactions from readers who find some of his views capricious and reactionary. However, the radical quality of Abbey's ideals also accounts for his popularity among many environmentalists. In *Resist Much, Obey Little* (1985), for example, Wendell Berry has written that "the trouble . . . with Mr. Abbey—a trouble, I confess, that I am disposed to like—is that he speaks insistently as himself." Abbey speaks most insistently as himself, perhaps, in what he calls his favorite essay in the book, "Immigration and Liberal Taboos" (pp. 41–44), an essay that has been labeled xenophobic by some, racist by others (Abbey argues that illegal immigrants are a "hungry, ignorant, unskilled, and culturally-morally-genetically impoverished people"). Though partially forgivable in the context of Abbey's larger work, these kinds of statements have disturbing implications for those avocating reasonable and workable solutions to the very real problems surrounding immigration and over-population. At their best, they critically inspire ecological activity, the preservation of person, place and culture; at their worst, they are little more than exercises in literary self-indulgence.

3. **Acquaviva, S.S. The Decline of the Sacred in Industrial Society.** London, England: Basil Blackwell, 1979. 289 pages.

As society shifts from agriculture to industry in its primary means of production, there occurs concrete changes in the way humans experience nature. In Western society, these changes in perception have influenced cultural belief, social organization, and religious identity—nature becoming less and less identifiable with the sacred. In this seminal work, Acquaviva, a professor of sociology at Padua University, traces the evolution of religious identity from the late Middle Ages to modern industrial society. He concludes that the process of desacralization coincides with "[t]he penetration of technology into all sectors of social life," that irreligiosity has its most discernible origins in "urbanization and industrialization" (p. 151). For a better understanding of how rural and urban environments maintain or discourage the religious self, this is an indispensable text. Extensive annotated notes.

4. **Adler, Margot. Drawing Down the Moon: The Resurgence of Paganism in America.** Boston, MA: Beacon Press, 1986. 595 pages.

Margot Adler, a staff reporter for National Public Radio, is also an activist concerned with ecological ritual and eco-feminist spirituality. This book, a revised edition, is one of the most comprehensive studies available on the religious psychology of neo-paganism, pagan nature worship, and eco-feminist ritual.

Drawing Down the Moon should be of interest to most feminist, ecological groups in general, religious historians, and followers of the pagan "occult." Adler does an excellent job of destroying many of the stereotypical images of contemporary neo-pagan practice; her informed analysis of this phenomenon should be of importance to those seeking a religious understanding of pagan folk custom, polytheistic animism, and natural living in general. The book contains three informative appendixes: "Ritual," "Proclamations," and "Resources": the latter being an extensive compendium of newsletters, books, and council groups that deal specifically with the study and practice of paganism old and new.

5. **Alford, C. Fred. Science and the Revenge of Nature: Marcuse and Habermas.** Gainesville, FL: The University Presses of Florida, 1985. 226 pages.

The domination of nature and the suppression of human nature were the central concerns of the first generation of critical theorists. In response to these concerns, the critical theorists attempted to create a non-instrumental understanding of the human and natural lifeworlds. Such an understanding was developed by Max Horkheimer and Theodor Adorno in the *Dialectic of Enlightenment* (1972) and later refined by Herbert Marcuse in *Eros and Civilization* (1955) and *One-Dimensional Man* (1964).

Jürgen Habermas, the self-appointed heir to the Frankfurt School, and whose social and critical philosophy has become virtually an industry here in the United States, does not, per se, continue this tradition. According to Habermas, nature can be known only through the two "species interests" of mankind: the technical cognitive interests in the control of nature and the practical cognitive interests in communication. Under the rubric of technical cognitive interests Habermas argues that the "human species persists over time only because it is capable of apprehending the world as a place to be manipulated and controlled" (p. 6). This interest therefore fixes how nature can be known to man.

According to Alford, because Habermas limits the ways in which we may know the world, nature can be known cognitively only through the technical cognitive interests. Habermas sees nature only as a means to human ends, his instrumental orientation toward nature is unapologetically anthropocentric. Throughout the text, Alford does an excellent job of unpacking Habermas' position on the issue while remaining true to the concerns of the first-generation Frankfurt School. (In the final analysis Alford interprets Marcuse's New Science as "superior" to Habermas'.) This work is definitely one of the most rigorous analyses to date on the place of science and nature in the Frankfurt School corpus. Alford's work provides critical insights for those interested in the role of reason in the creation of an ecological ethos.

6.   Alihen, Milla Aissa. Social Ecology: A Critical
     Analysis. New York, NY: Cooper Square,
     1964. 267 pages.

Originally published by Columbia University Press in 1938, this frequently ignored study offers one of the earliest critiques of human ecology as an empirical discipline. The work concerns itself with the relationship between community and society, and society and the natural order. The merger of the social and biological sciences in the 1920's, argues Alihen, did *not* "ecologize" sociology, nor correctly incorporate the human into nature's biotic community. Alihen insists that simply applying environmental metaphors to human or group life does not constitute an adequate discipline of ecology. Though apparently intended for an audience of social scientists of that period, *Social Ecology* continues to provide an excellent overview on the origins and historical evolution of human and social ecology. Additionally, it illustrates the early influence of ecology on both the natural and social sciences.

7.   Anglemyer, Mary, and Seagraves, Eleanor, et al.,
     comps. A Search for Environmental Ethics:
     An Initial Bibliography. Washington, D.C.:
     Smithsonian Institution Press, 1980. 119 pages.

     This annotated bibliography consists of 446 rather loosely organized
entries. The entries include articles, books, and monographs on topics related
to environmental ethics. It cites few philosophically oriented works and
therefore contains only a limited number of titles dealing with important ethical issues raised by recent environmental philosophy. Despite the philosophical omissions, the entries that are annotated are done with careful attention
to the relevancy of each work to the task at hand. Anglemyer, et al., know
the difference between wheat and chaff; the reader is given an economical
yet informative synopsis of each entry (most of the entries exceed seventy-
five words). However, while helpful, this intitial bibliography falls short of
its intended goal, which was to provide crux resource material in an informed
search for an environmental ethic. Titles are listed alphabetically, indexed
numerically. Sponsored by the Rachel Carson Council, Inc., Washington,
D.C.

8.   Anglemyer, Mary, and Seagraves, Eleanor R.,
     comps. The Natural Environment: An
     Annotated Bibliography on Attitudes and
     Values. Washington, D.C.: Smithsonian
     Institution Press, 1984. 268 pages.

     The companion volume to the previously reviewed text, this bibliography
contains 857 entries not included in the earlier work. It has corrected many
of the shortcomings of *A Search for Environmental Ethics* (1980) by including more titles related to contemporary ecophilosophy. However, the virtual
explosion in ecophilosophical literature makes this book, published in 1984,
partially obselete, i.e., major works such as Paul Taylor's *Respect for Nature*
(1986), Holmes Rolston's *Environmental Ethics* (1988), and Alston Chase's
Playing God in Yellowstone (1986) are missing. Despite this and other minor
problems, both books, taken together, provide an invaluable introduction to
the available literature on environmental ethics and philosophy.

9.   Ashby, Eric. Reconciling Man with the
     Environment. Leon Sloss Junior Memorial
     Lectures for 1977. Stanford, CA: Stanford
     University Press, 1978. 104 pages.

     A Cambridge biologist discusses the social values, public issues and
political processes surrounding environmental protection. Each of the three
lectures argues that there are current trends which point toward a shift from
exploitation of nature to symbiosis with nature. These trends, says Ashby, are

being converted into political activities with profound implications for future public policy concerns. In the end Ashby argues that even though environmental reconciliation with nature is preferable, it is possible only if existing social and political systems are first transformed by public conscience and opinion. Bibliography, notes.

10. **Attfield, Robin. The Ethics of Environmental Concern.** New York, NY: Columbia Press, 1983. 220 pages.

This work is divided into two parts: "Problems and Traditions," a survey of Judeo-Christian attitudes toward nature; and "Applied Ethics," a discussion of a utilitarian moral theory. Attfield clearly believes that these two approaches, when taken together, provide the best framework for a substantive environmental ethic. Attfield's treatment and understanding of stewardship relies heavily on his belief that the Judeo-Christian tradition remains the most influential element for extrapolating an ethics of the environment. The author maintains that because we belong to a Western society, with a specific cultural heritage, we must rely on an understanding of environmental problems in the context of our shared traditions, "without resorting to the dubious and implausible expedient of introducing a new environmental ethic" (p. 34).

With this point in mind, Attfield begins constructing his environmental ethic by defining the axiological norms found in Judeo(196Christian values. Using the language of classical utilitarisianism, Attfield embraces consequentialism as the most likely method for formulating such an ethical system. Attfield does, in the end, modify his utilitarianism to fit his needs, concluding that morally, what matters most, is the furthering of the interests of all of god's living creatures.

11. **Avens, Roberts. The New Gnosis: Heidegger, Hillman, and Angels.** Dallas, TX: Spring Publications, 1984. 155 pages.

The New Gnosis seeks to introduce and defend a metaphysics that re-ensouls and re-personifies the world by 1) defining the existential parameters of a radical new way of perceiving reality, and 2) supporting a knowledge that is not "divorced from the known, the inner from the outer, the self from the world" (p. 109). Like the neo-Platonic man who saw his existence in light of an "imaginal" world-soul, the Swedenborgian Man of Heidegger's phenemenology or Hillman's archetypal psychology knows himself not of the world but *in* the world.

In the radical re-personification of the cosmos, believes the author, we replace the isolated and dislocated soul of modern man directly upon the face of nature. We have a human/nature writ as one, an ontology that *a fortiori* deconstructs the Western notion of being for a participatory and creative being "linked" directly to an ensouled and personified cosmos. This particular intersubjective image of humans and nature, though evident in the work of Owen Barfield and others, belongs more precisely to the philosophy of Personalism. To conceive of ourselves and the world around us as a personal or meaningful whole, is to recover the primordial insight of the personal mode of being—the "ultimate metaphysical category."

As Avens notes, personalism in philosophy is much more than a representational system. Thus, for Avens, the personal must intimately identify with ultimate reality, create an acute agreement between ideas in the mind and the laws of nature, and of "human imagination with the cosmic imagination." Writes the author: "What we have here is a kind of universal ecology. Everything in the cosmos interconnects with its immediate surroundings, and these surroundings with wider environs, until the world, the solar system, and the more are included. Things necessarily exist through each thing, and each thing is a reflection of the whole. But again, as Hillman insists, this is not a 'fuzzy pantheism' or a 'general adoration of nature.' Rather, the whole of nature is experienced, as in Blake, through 'that joyful scrutiny of detail, that intimacy of each with each such as lovers know'" (p. 26). Extensive notes.

12. **Bahro, Rudolph. From Red to Green: Interviews with the New Left Review.**
London, England: Verso Books, 1984.
208 pages.

A founding member of West Germany's Green Party appraises—in a series of taped interviews—the rise and evolution of Green politics out of its neo-Marxian roots. One of the best philosophical discussions, in English, on the policies and practices of West Germany's ecological party.

13. **Bahro, Rudolph. Building the Green Movement.** Philadelphia, PA: New Society Publishers, 1986. 219 pages.

Bahro's most recent attempt at defining the social, philosophical, and religious dimensions of the Green political movement. Bahro begins this slender text with position papers defending his radical ecology and utopian communalism. Essentially, he calls for (1) the decentralization of society, (2) the transformation of work, (3) a new spiritual awareness, and (4) a communal order that rejects what he calls our present "exterminous" society.

While most of Bahro's arguments are well thought out and well articulated, his discussions on spirituality suffer from a severe eclecticism: he lumps, for example, Lao-Tzu, Heraclitus, Hegel, and the Bagwan Rajneesh into the same metaphysical melting pot. Also, his apocalyptic images of the evils of the modern world advance an eschatalogy that—while bringing a sense of urgency to the present ecological crisis—promotes an irrational fear of more traditional expressions of religious experience. The text provides a limited treatment of Third World issues and curiously ignores the liberatory powers and local and regional municipalism. Despite these and other important omissions, the volume provides a nice blueprint for the Green movement both here and abroad.

14. **Bailes, Kendall E. Environmental History:**
Critical Essays in Comparative Perspective.
Lanham, MD: University Press of America,
1985. 697 pages.

Proceedings from an international conference on environmental history, held at the University of California, Irvine, in 1982. Contains more than thirty entries, from ten sessions, by some of the most respected scholars in the field. Participants include Donald Worster, Carolyn Merchant, Alfred Crosby, J. Donald Hughes, Clarence Glacken, Roderick Nash, and John Pettulla. The main themes of the conference are carefully summarized by Bailes in the book's introduction, who sees environmental history as an important and exciting frontier in historiographic research.

Of more direct interest to ecophilosophers is Bruce Piasecki's commentary on René Dubos, "Environmental Ambivalence: An Analysis of Implicit Dangers" (pp. 83–98). In this paper, Piasecki argues that Dubos' ecology is both misinformed and misleading. There is *not*, says Piasecki, an inherent tendency in humans to change the environment as Dubos often suggests in works like *Wooing the Earth* (1980) and *Celebrations of Life* (1981). Richard Franks paper is much harsher; he writes in his commentary that Dubos' work is a "classic example of ideology—a system of premises and arguments designed to justify existing [non-ecological] institutions and relations" (p. 102). Other relevant articles include Donald Grinde's commentary on Navajo ecology and government policy and J. Donald Hughes' examination of the chthonic perspective in ancient Western thought. A comprehensive and wide-ranging statement on the critical issues involved in contemporary environmental history. Extensive index. Notes.

15. **Barbour, Ian G. ed. Earth Might Be Fair:**
Reflections on Ethics, Religion, and Ecology.
Englewood Cliffs, NJ: Prentice Hall, 1972.
168 pages.

Among the earlier anthologies on the relationship of ecology to religion, science, and ethics. Includes essays by Frederick Ferré, "Explanation in Science and Theology" (pp. 14–32), Daniel Williams, "Changing Concepts of Nature" (pp. 48–61); and Barbour's own "Attitudes toward Nature and Technology" (pp. 146–168). Barbour's introduction to the text provides a good summary of each of the nine entries, categorized under three separate but not unrelated headings: "Philosophy and Science," "Theology and Ecology," and "Ethics and Technology." Though the book's interdisciplinary thrust is immediately apparent, its strength lies in its insistence upon a critical synthesis of religious, moral, and aesthetic experience—an ecological theology.

A theology of nature, according to Barbour, would resacralize nature as a knowable manifestation of a "greater" reality. Man's responsibility for nature lies in humanity's acceptance of the role of God's steward. "Man does not have absolute dominion, for he is responsible to God. 'The Earth is the Lord's' because he created it. The land belongs ultimately to God, and man is only a trustee or steward. He is vice-regent, responsible for the welfare of those entrusted to him" (p. 149). On the theory of stewardship vs. dominion in Judeo-Christian thinking, Barbour concludes that while crucial differences exist, the recognition of Gods immanence in nature, the recognition that all forms of life are interdependent, evokes the most authentic vision for a socially viable ecological ethic.

16. **Barbour, Ian G. ed. Western Man and Environmental Ethics: Attitudes toward Nature and Technology.** Reading, MA: Addison-Wesley, 1973. 276 pages.

This collection of essays by Lynn White, Jr., René Dubos, Leo Marx, Wendell Berry, Paul Goodman and others, continues the dominion vs. stewardship debate initiated in Barbour's *Earth Might Be Fair* (1972). The book begins with Lynn White's now infamous "The Historical Roots of our Ecological Crisis" (pp. 18–30) and ends with Jorgen Randers and Donella Meadows' "The Carrying Capacity of Our Global Environment: A Look at Ethical Alternatives" (pp. 253–276). There are also excellent entries by Gabriel Farkre, "Ecology and Theology" (pp. 116–131) and the now defunct writing collective *Ecology Action East*, "The Power to Destroy the Power to Create" (pp. 243–252). While many of the readings do examine attitudes toward nature and technology, most concern the doctrine of creation or the theology of ecology.

17. **Barbour, Ian G. Technology, Environment, and Human Values.** New York, NY: Praeger, 1980. 332 pages.

A well-documented work of thirteen chapters, Barbour's book is divided into three parts. Part one looks at the relationship of technology to attitudes toward nature, part two surveys current environmental policy and politics. Part Three is a discussion of global issues of scarcity and Third World food shortages. The format, along with Barbour's straightforward style, places the work in the "textbook" genre, however. Provides some excellent resource material, as well as a concise introduction to the many types of ethical theory in the different approaches to contemporary environmental ethics. Extensive notes.

18. **Barfield, Owen. Saving the Appearances: A Study in Idolatry.** New York, NY: Harcourt Brace Jovanovich, 1965. 190 pages.

In Barfield's opinion, we can understand the origin of original thought, i.e., participation, only by going back "to the ages when men were conscious, not merely in their heads, but in the beating of their hearts, and the pulsing of their blood—when thinking was not merely *of* Nature, but was Nature itself" *(Poetic Diction: A Study in Meaning*, 1971, p. 81).

In *Saving the Appearances*, Barfield outlines his metaphysics of participation; the ontology of "the extrasensory relation between man and the phenomenon" (p. 40). This intersubjectivity between subject and object, argues Barfield, has profound implications for understanding the world we presently find ourselves. In a nonparticipating consciousness, knowledge is acquired by actually recognizing the distance between ourselves and nature. Prehistorical consciousness, on the other hand, requires any representation of the "other" to be inexorably linked to a part of me. Barfield's deconstruction of the ontology of modern appearances, the disparity between seeing and believing, fact and value, provides the basis for a challenging reinterpretation of our relationship to science, religion, and nature. An invaluable text for the ecophilosopher.

19. **Barnette, Henlee H. The Church and the Ecological Crisis.** Grand Rapids, MI: Eerdmans, 1972. 114 pages.

Barnette asserts that the traditional Christian approach to nature has been a major contributing factor to ecological destruction. The overemphasis on "otherworldliness," says the author, has led to a disregard and even exploitation of the physical world. As a steward of God's creation, humanity must realign its present relationship to the biosphere. Dominion over nature does not mean the right to exploit nature but to establish nature as God's covenant. "I establish my Covenant with you, and with your seed after you and with every living thing." Whether or not the stewardship vision advanced by Barnette is, ecologically speaking, a question of too little, too late remains to be seen. Nonetheless, there are several books that better address the stewardship issue. See, for example, Joranson and Butigan, *Cry of the Environment* (1984) and Wesley Granberg–Michaelson, *A Worldly Spirituality* (1984).

20. **Barrett, William. The Illusion of Technique.**
Garden City, NY: Anchor Books, 1979.
173 pages.

In a pervasively technologized culture, the role of technique in shaping our understanding of nature becomes, even in philosophy, an inescapable problematic. The illusion of technique pervades all methods of inquiry. Here the author warns of the dangers of circumventing human activity with the development and application of technique to all forms of human experience. The epilogue to this work, briefly but beautifully written, describes the place of nature in contemporary philosophical discourse. Barrett puzzles over the lack of any concern for nature in the work of Sartre, while congratulating Whitehead, Bergson, and Merleau-Ponty for attempting to come to terms with "the vast organic world of animals, plants, insects, and protozoa, with whom our life is linked in a single history" (p. 335). Notes, bibliography.

21. **Barrett, William. Death of the Soul: From Descartes to the Computer.** New York, NY: Anchor/Doubleday, 1986. 173 pages.

William Barrett, currently Distinguished Professor of Philosophy at Pace University, is widely known as one of the first philosophers to introduce existentialism to the United States. In this work he critiques contemporary philosophy as being preoccupied with disembodied data and theoretical exactitude, which, as he sees it, ignores the more important existential concerns of religious spirituality: the life of the human soul. In chapter 9 Barrett offers an intelligent critique of philosophical and literary deconstruction, the textcentric philosophy of Jacques Derrida and other practitioners of what he calls "the desubstantiation of being" (pp. 127–141). Contemporary philosophers are products of a technological age, argues Barrett, whose theories of subjectivity are removed from any clear religious understanding of substantial, historical being. The computerization of consciousness, like deconstruction, also helps to advance an understanding of the self (read: soul) as a string of meaningless and simulated symbols; it does nothing to resurrect the organic body of nature into a single unified vision of substantial reality.

22. **Baruchello, Gianfranco, and Martin, Henry. How to Imagine: A Narrative on Art, Agriculture and Creativity.** New York, NY: McPherson, 1984. 143 pages.

Modern art theory generally ignores things living and organic: the aesthetic dimension of the modern artist is seldom juxtaposed with the sensibilities of ecological concerns. Fortunately, recent literature has tried to unify these two important issues, and this particular book represents one of the best attempts of doing so. In Baruchello's words, "I wanted to start looking at things more clearly, and in doing so, I really began to get interested in the soil, in the earth, in everything connected with them that was going on around me. I began to understand the possibilities of a different order of reflection that the situation here might offer me, an order of reflection at a much higher level of reality" (pp. 52–53). *How to Imagine* is a spirited and topical narrative of taped and edited conversations of artist/farmer Gianfranco Baruchello and American journalist Henry Martin. Extends and touches upon a diverse range of topics: Duchamp, lettuce, the soul, sugar beets, animal husbandry, feminism, technology, and politics.

23. **Bates, Marston. The Forest and the Sea: A Look at the Economy of Nature and the Ecology of Man.** New York, NY: Random House, 1960. 278 pages.

One of the earliest narratives on the relationship between the ecology of nature and the ecology of humans. This book is unusual in that it does provide indepth discussions of our relationship to aquatic life, the diverse ecology of streams, rivers, and oceans. The concluding chapter, entitled "Man's Place in Nature" (pp. 246–262), summarizes some of Bates' ethical, aesthetic, and utilitarian reasons for preserving nature's diversity. We should preserve nature, writes Bates, because "it is morally the right thing to do; it will provide, for future generations, a richer and more satisfying experience than would otherwise be possible " (p. 262). What some consider the classic ecological text, Bates' book is today a fairly standard reading of the ecological sensibility.

24. **Bateson, Gregory. Steps to an Ecology of Mind.** New York, NY: Ballantine Books, 1972. 517 pages.

The mind/nature dichotomy has always played an important role in Batesonian epistemology. In *Steps to an Ecology of Mind*, a collection of previously published essays and lectures, Bateson tells us that Western science has wrongly attempted to build the bridge between form and substance, mind and nature. For Bateson, the reality of the mind/nature relationship is understood as immanent *only* in the *arrangement* and *behavior* of phenomena, not necessarily inherent in matter itself. So unlike ecophilosopher Owen Barfield, Bateson argues that there is no sacred participation, animism, or "greater reality" in the ontological human/nature relationship, only a holistic *system* that reflects the true dialectical process between self and form, substance and nature. In most respects, this paradigm for knowing, because it relies heavily on the processual terminology of cybernetic systems theory, reduces our apprehension of nature to metacommunicated "codes" or disembodied cybernetic "structures."

Though many have argued, ecophilosophically speaking, that the early work of Bateson contains one of the most sophisticated epistemologies for resolving the mind/nature dichotomy, one must conclude that Bateson's epistemology, despite its inherent organicism, partially diminishes nature to an ecology of *mind*, mechanical in content, Cartesian in origin. Preface by Mark Engel.

25. **Bateson, Gregory. Mind and Nature: A Necessary Unity.** New York, NY: E. P. Dutton, 1979. 238 pages.

While there is still some authentic ecological holism in *Steps to an Ecology of Mind* (1972), this latter work by Bateson continues the mechanization of the self: nature has become more and more of a disembodied entity, entrapped in a universe of processual mechanisms or "metapatterns." In sum, nature, in *Mind and Nature*, becomes less of an equal focus of concern; the theories of Bateson begin to dissolve the living and breathing world into a series of reflexive psychological structures (mind over matter!). Even Bateson's description of the "circuitry of mentation" is couched in terms of a nonlocatable "milieu of events"—set in motion by no one, understood not as much by the existence of objects or events as much as by their *absence*.

In some respects, Bateson's logic of mentation reminds one of the Derridean project of *différence*—in which the ontological traces, not the images themselves, reflect the true nature of unfolded reality. Felt participation no longer exists on its own terms, because nature can be known only *analogically*; in the binary system of referential codes. (See especially chapter 4, "Mental Process.") Appendix. Glossary of terms.

26. **Bergon, Frank, ed. The Wilderness Reader.** New York, NY: New American Library, 1980. 372 pages.

An excellent anthology on the place of humans and human society in wilderness. The entries include writings from a cross section of noted explorers, scientists, historians, and politicians, including: William Byrd, William Bartram, Meriwether Lewis, George Catlin, John James Audubon, Francis Parkman, and John Muir.

27. **Berman, Morris. The Reenchantment of the World.** Ithaca, NY: Cornell University Press, 1981. 357 pages. (Paperback edition, New York: Bantam Books, 1984).

Berman's survey studies the content and emergence of the modern scientific *Weltanshauung*. Though this work provides yet another important critique of the mechanistic Cartesian worldview, the most provocative section of the book (chapters 5 and 6) deals not with Descartes, but with the metaphysics of humanity's corporeal embodiment in the organic world. Drawing heavily from the work of Michael Polanyi, Wilhelm Reich, and Ashley Montagu, Berman lays out in this section the tacit epistemological foundations for an empathetic and participatory science. Tomorrow's metaphysics must reject the mechanistic thought patterns of postmodern society and embrace the virtues of visceral and "noncognitive" knowing, writes Berman.

Though portions of this book are perhaps too preoccupied with systems thought and Batesonian cybernetics, the conclusion drawn is an important one: unless the cybernetic dream of the 21st century is replaced with an ecological dream that seeks the biotic resubmersion of humanity into the environment, there can be no reenchantment(and thus preservation) of the world—only a world of progressive disenchantment, personal despair, and ecological catastrophe. Extensive notes. Glossary of terms.

28. **Berry, Thomas. Teilhard in the Ecological Age.**
Chambersburg, PA: Anima Books, 1982.
33 pages.

A re-interpretation of the writings of Teilhard de Chardin in conjunction with contemporary ecological principles and attitudes. In this booklet, Berry, the president of the American Teilhardian Association for the Future of Man, argues that Teilhard's humanistic and "creative transformation" of nonhuman nature allows for a mode of being that establishes an ideal intercommunication between self and the total earth community—establishes a communion that allows humans to live "lightly on the earth" (pp. 18, 25). Because of an alleged anthropocentric bias, Berry's (and Teilhard's) position is considered flawed by some ecophilosophers. The "creative transformation of nature by humans," it is argued, only continues to invite the domination of nature (and humans). Nevertheless, this is an important position paper on the place of Teilhardian philosophy in contemporary environmental ethics.

29. **Berry, Thomas. The Dream Of The Earth.**
San Francisco, CA: Sierra Club Books, 1988.
256 pages.

As all great utopian thinkers know, imagination plays an essential role in shaping concrete human reality. Today's dream is tomorrow's lived–world. Father Berry, whose work has influenced a number of environmental thinkers (including Charlene Spretnak) provides his own unique vision of an ecological tomorrow. Utilizing studies from both the human and natural sciences, the author discusses the idea of the sacred in the context of aesthetic, imaginative, and creative experiences. Our ecological visions must embody these principles if they are to effectively transform the pervasive industrial order, says Berry. A sustainable future cannot be created entirely from cultural traditions, nor from a complete rejection of the past. Additional chapters focus on the concept of bioregionalism, patriarchy, the historical role of the American Indian, and "the American College in the ecological age." Annotated bibliography (153 entries).

30. **Berry, Wendell. The Unsettling of America:**
Culture and Agriculture. San Francisco, CA:
Sierra Club Books, 1977. 228 pages.

A farmer, conservationist, poet, and educator critiques the many disparities of modern industrial society. Berry, the author of several books related to ecophilosophical issues, e.g., *Standing by Words* (1983), *The Gift of Good Land* (1981), and *A Continuous Harmony* (1972), argues that we need to return to a profound "sense of place"—we need to be more than simply users of the land. Berry's stewardship position defends small-scale organic farming techniques, the virtues of alternative "land-use" methods. In this important, highly influential work, Berry cites the Amish and Mennonite communities as examples of small farmers who maintain thriving, proficient farms, yet satisfying, ecologically rewarding lifestyles. Community and Agriculture. Notes.

31. **Berry, Wendell. Home Economics.**
San Francisco, CA: North Point Press, 1987.
192 pages.

Fourteen essays, dating from 1982, on themes ranging from the virtues of wilderness and the family farm, to the intrinsic value of community and rural culture. The book's title originates in the Greek term for economics, *oikonomikós*, which refers to the management or stewardship of household. Though the idea is perhaps dealt with most directly in the essay entitled "Two Economies" (pp. 54–75), all fourteen essays in some way refer to this central theme.

The two selections "Getting Along with Nature" (pp. 6–20) and "Preserving Wilderness" (pp. 137–151) should be of primary interest to ecophilosophical studies as Berry summarizes his views on peopled and unpeopled landscapes. In short, the author sees culture as heavily embedded in unspoiled wilderness while simultaneously rising above it. In this respect, preserving wilderness in "preserves" or National Forests does not alone ensure the perpetuation of such areas. To truly conserve wilderness, proclaims Berry, we need to create economies and values in a *culture* that promotes wise use of our natural resources. The question, then, is not one of "humans" vs. "nature" or "homocentricism" vs. "biocentrism." It is simply one of emphasis on culturally derived values in the natural world.

32. **Bilsky, Lester J. Historical Ecology and Social Change.** Port Washington, N.Y.: Kennikat Press, 1980. 195 pages.

An important study of environmental crises both past and present, this anthology contains a number of important essays on historical ecology and environmental history. Part one examines the fundamental factors and methodologies of historical ecology, focusing on the work of biologists, geographers, and anthropologists—the models they have developed in dealing with ecological issues. Part two examines the ecology of the ancient world, J. Donald Hughes' essay "Early Greek and Roman Environmentalists" merits considerable mention here (pp. 45–59). Part three presents various religious and secular attitudes toward nature in the European Middle Ages: the ecological crisis of fourteenth century Europe is discussed aptly in an essay by Charles Bowlus (pp. 86–99), for example. The final section, chapters 8 through 10, traces the history of modern ecology, concluding with John Culbertson's essay, "Ecology, Economics, and the Quality of Life" (pp. 156–170). Contains an invaluable bibliography listing of over 150 titles, categorized as follows: "Environmental History: General Works," "Ecological Crises in Prehistory," "Ecological Crises in Classical Antiquity," "Ecological Crises in Ancient China," "Environmental History of Post-Medieval Europe," "The Environment in the United States," "Environmental History and Economic Theory."

33. **Birch, Charles, and Cobb, John B. The Liberation of Life: From Cell to the Community.** Cambridge, MA: Cambridge University Press, 1983. 353 pages.

An ambitious book that begins by focusing on the ontological issues raised by molecular ecology, population ecology, and organismic ecology and concludes with the authors' suggestion that the "ecological model" of life represents the most adequate view for understanding our present natural (and human) order.

The authors, a process theologian and an Australian biologist, claim they are interested in the liberation of *all* life: their arguments maintain that the liberation of nature must concomitantly foster the liberation of humanity. Their position follows the process philosophies of Alfred North Whitehead and Charles Hartshorne, and thus maintains a graded hierarchy of value among sentient and non-sentient beings. Today, they argue, most people are captives of a metaphysics which tends to objectify the natural world in both its human and non-human aspects. The "liberation of life" would overcome the objectifying character of Western civilization because the liberation of social structures and human behavior "will involve a shift from manipulation and management of living creatures, human and non-human alike, to respect for its life (nature) in its fullness" (p. 2). This "eco-praxis," say the authors, would create a sensitivity to the interrelatedness of biological and human events; create the responsibility of re-sacralizing social and personal activity so that all living creatures may develop accordingly.

34. **Blackstone, William T., ed. Philosophy and Environmental Crisis.** Athens, GA: University of Georgia Press, 1974. 140 pages.

An eight–essay anthology consisting of papers given at the Fourth Annual Conference in Philosophy at the University of Georgia, February 18–20, 1971. Begins with a discussion by Eugene Odum on the conceptual and normative implications of the environmental crisis and ends with Pete Gunter's "The Big Thicket"; a case study of attitudes toward the environment in the southeastern United States (pp. 117–132).

"The Big Thicket" is the southeastern evergreen forest that once swept from southern Virginia to central Florida and westward to eastern Texas. Gunter outlines the ecological history of this once enormous "ecotome," concluding that it was primarily the utilitarian use values of industry that initiated the widespread destruction of this unique bioregion. Other essays by William Blackstone, "Ethics and Ecology" (pp. 16–42), Charles Hartshorne, "The Environmental Results of Technology" (pp. 69–78), and Walter O'Briant, "Man, Nature, and the History of Philosophy" (pp. 79–89).

35. **Bly, Robert. News of the Universe: Poems of Twofold Consciousness.** San Francisco, CA: Sierra Club Books, 1980. 305 pages.

A collection of poems which illuminate the relationship of individual human consciousness to nature. Robert Bly, himself an accomplished poet, has arranged and edited this volume, selecting poems by Blake, Yeats, Whitman, D. H. Lawrence, Gary Snyder, Goethe, Rilke, Novalis, and many others. Each of the six parts opens with a short but invocative essay by Bly, who emphasizes the inner and outer aspects of human consciousness as well as the possible union of the two in a pre-technological, pre-Cartesian relationship to nature. Over 150 poems drawn from both Western and non–Western sources.

36. **Bonifazi, Conrad. The Soul of the World: An Account of the Inwardness of Things.** Lanham, MD: University Press of America, 1978. 243 pages.

A Christian theologian and Teilhard de Chardinian scholar, Bonifazi wants to reassert the sacredness of nature by relating "ecological consciousness" to the radical Christian pantheism of personalistic spirituality. Bonifazi's position has, however, been criticized as being anthropocentric and un-reluctantly humancentered; his metaphysics has been said to place nature's body solely in the psyche of human beings. Bonifazi's emphasis on Chardinian transformational psychology does seem to relegate the *anima mundi* directly to human consciousness: "[t]he earth is a psycho-somatic entity. Its psyche, extending from the biosphere, is principally concentrated in human beings" (p. 232). Admittedly, the "man perfecting nature" attitude is prevalent throughout the Judeo-Christian tradition; but does radically personalizing nature always qualitatively anthropocentrize it? It seems a far more complicated issue, and one that warrants further investigation. This book provides an excellent departure point for such a study.

37. **Bookchin, Murray. Toward an Ecological Society.** Montreal: Black Rose Books, 1980. 313 pages.

A collection of a dozen essays that critically relate Bookchin's understanding of ecology to the society in which we now find ourselves. *Toward an Ecological Society* is unique in that it anticipates the separation of "shallow" environmentalism from deep critical issues and possibilities of human liberation. The problematic is best explained in Bookchin's lengthy critique of André Gorz's *Ecology as Politics* (1980), in the appendix to this text (pp. 289–313). Other essays provide striking condemnations of Marxist reformism as "the culmination of bourgeois Enlightenment" (p. 195). Marxism, argues Bookchin, "converges with Enlightenment bourgeois ideology at a point where both seem to share a scientistic conception of reality . . . " (p. 197). This scientistic conception, adds the author, renders nature simply as an "object" to be used by "man" and consequently despiritualizes both humanity and nature.

In the chapter entitled "The Concept of Ecotechnologies and Ecocommunities" (pp. 99–112), Bookchin looks at both the historical and philosophical roots of human scale technology and organization. Here, he persuasively argues that liberatory technology differs in both scale and application from purely instrumental notions of technique. Moreover, the technological system is not a neutral instrument that can be used for good or evil ends, nor is it an autonomously evolving determinant of social change in all institutions. In Bookchin's analysis, tools, machines, and techniques "are immersed in a social world of human intentions, needs, wills, and interactions" (p. 128). To conclude, these essays, which span nearly a decade of the author's work, illustrate the profound social and political promise of ecology as both a theory and practice. Notes.

38. **Bookchin, Murray. The Ecology of Freedom: The Emergence and Dissolution of Hierarchy.** Palo Alto, CA: Cheshire Books, 1982. 385 pages.

The most definitive statement in ecological literature on the legacy of freedom in organic society. The realm of human freedom, insists the author, resides in humanity's dialectical relationship to the natural world. It is only in the human/nature dialectic that we can begin to understand the bonds of domination and oppression in Western culture. Bookchin, the critical ecologist *par excellence*, and one of the founders of the modern ecophilosophy movement, provides in this work one of the most devastating critiques of the modern institution of domination and control, the hierarchical origins of morality that emerge out of what he calls the "epistemologies of rule."

In chapter 3, "The Emergence of Hierarchy" (pp. 62–88), Bookchin says that only with the emergence of the domination of human by human could the logic of the domination of nature arise. One of the earliest examples he gives is the rise of patriarchal morality in late Neolithic society. It is here where one clearly sees the beginnings of the domination of nature. "Even before man embarks on his conquest of man—of class by class—patriarchal morality obliges him to affirm his conquest of women. The subjugation of her nature and its absorption into the nexus of patriarchal morality forms the archetypal act of domination that ultimately gives rise to man's imagery of a subjugated nature. It is perhaps not accidental that nature and earth retain the female gender into our own time. What may seem to us like linguistic atavism that reflects a long ago era when social life was matricentric and nature was its domestic abode may well be an ongoing and subtly viable expression of man's continual violation of woman as nature and nature as women" (p. 121). Social Ecology. Notes.

39. **Bookchin, Murray. The Modern Crisis.** Philadelphia, PA: New Society Publishers, 1985. 167 pages.

A collection of five introductory essays that presents Bookchin's thinking on social ecology, moral economics, ecological and social reconstruction, nature and society. Contents include: "Rethinking Ethics, Nature, and Society" (pp. 1–48), "What Is Social Ecology?" (pp. 49–76), "Market Economy or Moral Economy?" (pp.77–97), and "An Appeal for Social and Ecological Sanity" (pp. 99–164). A learned and accessible statement by one of the founders of the ecophilosophy movement.

40. **Bookchin, Murray. The Rise of Urbanization and the Decline of Citizenship.**

San Francisco, CA: Sierra Club Books, 1987.
300 pages.

An analysis outlining the author's major thoughts on the social, psychological, and political aspects of urbanization. In this long-in-the-making work (ten years), Bookchin looks at the cities of both ancient and modern civilization, their ecological merits and downfalls. In critiquing the modern cityscape, Bookchin offers possible ways in which we might transcend the urban *ethos* without necessarily losing some of its original organic and social sensibilities. In chapter 8, "The New Municipal Agenda" (pp. 225–288), Bookchin celebrates the New England town meeting as the exemplary model of eco-communitarian democracy in practice. Here, in this concluding chapter, he discusses the eco-political organization of grassroots assemblies, advocating local municipalism as the most practical forum for advancing Green ideas and principles. A richly documented, historically grounded volume. Notes.

41. Brooks, Paul. Speaking for Nature: How Literary Naturalists from Henry Thoreau to Rachel Carson Have Shaped America.
Boston, MA: Houghton Mifflin, 1980.
304 pages.

American naturalists have not only had a passionate concern for preserving the natural world but a gift for writing about it. Henry David Thoreau, John Muir, Mary Austin, Aldo Leopold, Rachel Carson, and a host of others have led the fight to protect the American environment as much from their words as from their deeds. The influence of the literary naturalist on the political, popular, and ecological heritage of America is the primary focus of this biographical narrative. Writes the author: "America's interest in nature goes back to the earliest days of the republic. Since that time, owing largely to the work of our popular nature writers, this interest has spread throughout our society to the point where a unique wild area or rare species of bird or mammal is valued as a manmade work of art. In short, appreciation of nature has become a part of our national heritage" (p. xi).

In *Speaking for Nature*, Brooks writes equally well about our literary naturalists' philosophical and ethical positions, making a number of critical observations about their changes in attitudes and values—their changing approaches to nature—over the past several hundred years. An important book in that it illustrates the active role of literature in shaping environmental attitudes. Contains an "Index for Further Reading," listing recommended books by each of the many authors cited in the text. American Environmental History. American Naturalists.

42. **Brown, Lester. Building a Sustainable Society.**
New York, NY: Norton, 1981. 433 pages.

For over a decade the Washington-based research group known as Worldwatch Institute has been analyzing global problems. Lester Brown, the director of that institute, has published several books (and dozens of position papers) that resonate with a deep appreciation for ecological solutions to those same global problems. *World Without Borders* (1972), *By Bread Alone* (1974), and *The Twenty-Ninth Day* (1978) are three volumes worthy of mention; each suggests a need to radically alter our use of the world's resources. Though Brown's books are often overfilled with reductionistic empirical data and a pragmatic, energy-centric understanding of the gifts-of-nature, his efforts provide valuable evidence for the feasibility of alternative "ecological" modes of social organization and production—modes that may not be profoundly ecological in the existential sense, but nevertheless may direct our values toward more equitable, more sustainable ways of ordering our communities. The last chapter of this book does, in fact, attempt to deal with the issue of values, arguing that our priorities must shift from an ethic of materialism to an ethic of voluntary simplicity. "Perhaps more than any other ethic," says Brown, "voluntary simplicity reconciles the needs of the person, the community, the economy, and the environment" (p. 355). Notes.

43. **Buber, Martin. Paths in Utopia.** Translated by
R.F.C. Hull, Boston, MA: Beacon Press, 1958.
152 pages.

Recent studies have illustrated the many similarities between ecological and utopian thought (See, e.g., Rudolf Moos and Robert Brownstein, *Environment and Utopia*, 1977). In this study, religious philosopher Martin Buber provides an informed history of the utopian ideal from Saint-Simon and Fourier to Karl Marx and Lenin. After three, generally introductory discussions, chapters 4, 5, and 6 provide detailed critical analyses of the utopian theories of Proudhon, Kropotkin, and Gustav Landauer, respectively. The four remaining chapters look at a variety of utopian experiments: the revolutionary socialism of Marx and Lenin; the crisis within our own present social order; the importance of the Jewish *kibbutz* as an alternative to less communitarian social arrangements. If environmental and utopian thinking are to be brought together—merged in a coherent synthesis—an acute understanding of the evolution of utopian ideas is needed. Buber's classic study no doubt supplies the reader with the appropriate tools for future speculation about the relationship between ecological and communitarian structures—the utopian dimensions they embody. Introduction by Ephraim Fischoff.

44. **Buber, Martin. I and Thou.** Translated by
    Ronald Gregor Smith. 2nd ed. New York, NY:
    Charles Scribner's Sons, 1958. 137 pages.

In all of his work, Martin Buber's dominant theme concerns the relationship of oneself to the world, other men, and God. First written in 1922, *I and Thou* discusses the existential differences of participated being and objectified "otherness." Buber contrasts the objective being of what he calls the "I–It" relationship with the reciprocal and intersubjective "I–Thou." The "I–Thou" relationship incorporates totally the "other" into one's being: a tree or person is no longer spoken of as an objectified "it," but as a participated "thou." In other words, because the "other" becomes an integral part of one's own subjective experience, there is no longer any ontological separation of the two subjects.

Recently this notion has been extended into the philosophical ecology literature where many ecophilosophers have created ethical stances based on Buber's intersubjective ontology. Many are saying that since we have reduced nature to an objectified "it," nature can no longer be understood as an integral part of human experience. And because we no longer identify with nature, we allow ourselves to manipulate, control, and exploit the ecosystem. The saying "you" or "thou" to nature would bring back the participatory being of a highly personal, highly ecological, human existence. Postscript.

45. **Buttimer, Ann, and Seamon, David, eds. The
    Human Experience of Space and Place.**
    London, England: Croom Helm, 1980.
    199 pages.

The editors, two phenomenological geographers, have collected a number of representative essays on the relationship of human experience to the "geography of the lifeworld." Seamon, who has written extensively on the relationship of phenomenology to environmental thought, begins the book with a useful introductory statement about phenomenological geography in general: "Phenomenology strives for the actualization of contact. As a way of study it seeks to meet the things in the world as those things in themselves and so describe them. Geography studies the earth as the dwelling place of man. As one of its tasks, it seeks to understand how people live in relation to everyday places, spaces, and environment. A phenomenological geography borrows from both fields of knowing and directs its attention to the essential nature of man's dwelling on earth. . . . A phenomenological geography asks the significance of people's inescapable immersion in a geographical world" (p. 148).

From a purely theoretical standpoint, the essays in this study do not stress the Husserlian claim that a purely phenomenological geography, an eidetic science, must provide the basis for the building of a sound empirical science of things geographical. The position here is more closely related to the phenomenological approach of Merleau-Ponty's; the distinction between eidetic and empirical sciences is de-emphasized.

46. **Caldwell, Lyton K. International Environmental Policy: Emergence and Dimensions. Durham, NC: Duke University Press, 1984. 367 pages.**

Like Caldwell's earlier volume *In Defense of Earth* (1972), this well researched synthesis examines, in depth, the growth of an international environmental ethic, the recent trend towards "the emergence of a new configuration of international environment policy" (p. 3). The author also looks at the various international organizations and agencies concerned with resource depletion, degradation, and abuse. Issues covered include: the transportation of hazardous materials, the atmosphere, bilateral and multi-lateral regional agreements, outerspace, and the standards of international litigation.

47. **Callicott, J. Baird, ed. Companion to a Sand County Almanac: Interpretive and Critical Essays. Madison, WI: University of Wisconsin Press, 1987. 308 pages.**

Aldo Leopold may prove to be the major figure of the twentieth century American conservation movement despite the fact that there are few, if any, sustained studies of his work. This particular collection of essays focuses primarily on Leopold's seminal *A Sand County Almanac*, providing a new and thoughtful analysis of that much read, albeit less philosophically appreciated, volume. Early reviews of the anthology in question have noted its exceptionally high quality, attributing this to the many accomplished contributors: Roderick Nash, Peter Fritzell, Susan Flader, Holmes Rolston, III, Wallace Stegner, and J. Baird Callicott are represented here. The editor (J. Baird Callicott) presents convincing arguments for the importance of this work in environmental philosophy, having, in 1971, used this text in what could have been the first Evironmental Ethics course of its kind.

The reviewer has a deeply felt appreciation for *Sand County*, having experienced the "sky dance" of the woodcock as a young boy in northwest Georgia. (My reading of Leopold's classic work coincided exactly with this profoundly moving event—see pages 30–34). Specific entries include Dennis Ribben's "The Making of *A Sand County Almanac*" (pp. 91–109), J. Baird Callicott's "The Conceptual Foundations of the Land Ethic" (pp. 186–119), John Tallmadge's "The Anatomy of a Classic" (pp. 110–127), Curt Meine's "Aldo Leopold's Early Years" (pp. 17–39), Susan Flader's "Aldo Leopold's

Sand County" (pp. 40–62), and Holmes Rolston's "Duties to Ecosystems" (pp. 246–275). Appendix.

48. **Capra, Fritjof. The Turning Point: Science, Society, and the Rising Culture.** New York, NY: Simon and Schuster, 1982. 464 pages.

Fritjof Capra is embraced by many ecophilosophers for his theoretical work in the "new physics;" his general critique of the Cartesian/Newtonian worldview. In *The Turning Point*, Capra continues his critique of this *Weltanshauung*, offering the reader a number of theoretical and philosophical alternatives to that approach.

The author argues that the Cartesian/Newtonian bias of today's life and social sciences—by isolating self from society, humanity from nature—not only separates the individual subject from the balanced unity of nature, but also ignores the dynamic interrelationship inherent in the earth organism: "We live today in a globally interconnected world, in which biological, psychological, social, and environmental phenomena are all interdependent. To describe this world appropriately, we need an ecological perspective which the Cartesian worldview does not offer" (p. 16).

The alternative ecological perspective which the author proceeds to describe is, in his words, a truly holistic vision of reality—*the systems view of life*—in which the "integrated web of living and nonliving forms are symbiotically married (p. 275). Capra devotes nearly one-fourth of this massive work to the existential virtues of the systems view of life, summarizing and expounding upon a number of the more popular theories: Ilya Prigogine, Ervin Laszlo, Erich Jantsch, Arthur Koestler, Jacques Monad, Gregory Bateson, and Karl Pribham are all integrated into Capra's eclectic version of "ecological holism."

What Capra does not seem to find problematic is that however reciprocal, dialectical, or ecological the systems view of life may first appear, the workings of nature or even human nature, are not reducible to such quasi-mechanistic frameworks. The systems view of nature is ultimately dependent on the mechanistic metaphors of the very science and physics it wants to reject. As an example, Capra no longer views physical reality as "discrete material" or "subatomic particles," but as a "constant flux or flow of energy transformations" (pp. 78–79). By simply emphasizing relationship over autonomy, one does not automatically create a holistic epistemology. Obviously, Capra wants to escape the world of the machine, but his championing of general systems theory makes his attempts to do so, less plausible.

49. **Capra, Fritjof, and Spretnak, Charlene. Green Politics: The Global Promise.** New York, NY: Dutton, 1984. 254 pages.

The German Green movement (Die Grünen) has played a small but important role in re-shaping world politics over the past ten years. For those unfamiliar with the party, the ideological pillars of Germany's Green politics include: ecology, social responsibility, grassroots democracy, and nonviolence. The authors of *Green Politics* provide a candid introduction to this movement as well as a critical assessment of the possible application of Germany's Green politics to America. The book's depth, however, is to be questioned as it often misreads the roles of Green leaders (for example Petra Kelly and Rudolf Bahro) in shaping the party's platform and philosophies. Since Green parties are and have been forming in almost every major country around the globe, *Green Politics* remains, nonetheless, a timely primer to the social and political virtues of ecological movements.

50. **Carson, Rachel. Silent Spring.** Boston, MA:
Houghton Mifflin, 1962. 368 pages.

An environmental classic. Since its publication some 25 years ago, *Silent Spring* remains one of the most important documents of environmental literature. An attack on human carelessness, greed and irresponsibility, Carson's jeremiad documents the ecological consequences of pollution, pesticides, and over-population. A heavily researched work that has been an inspiration for an entire generation of environmentalists. References.

51. **Catton, William R., Jr. Overshoot: The Ecological Basis of Revolutionary Change.**
Urbana, IL: University of Illinois Press, 1980.
298 pages.

Catton notes that the modern foundations of social relations have been undermined by an arrogance in exaggerating the difference between self and other creatures, between human history and natural history. Contemporary society ignores the basic principles and laws of ecology—it steals from the future in order to maintain an overproductive present. In order to maintain the basic necessities of life for all peoples, argues Catton, we must maintain nature's "carrying capacity" by nurturing a consciousness that would internalize the basic principles and laws of ecology (e.g., succession, niche, symbiosis, etc.)

Though Catton's arguments are well formulated, it is sometimes difficult to find the point where the human and natural worlds meet in his neo Malthusian styled polemic. Moreover, carrying capacity is an ambiguous and relevant term: societies that seemingly do not live under accepted laws of succession or niche often sustain highly ecological lifestyles and do very little damage to their environment. Carrying capacity is often transcended, or at least extended, by humans who "undermine" the laws of nature through mutual aid and cooperation. In addition, the simple reduction of *human* ecology to iron clad natural laws often ignores the latent potentialities within the ecological *social* human and thus has very little to say about how such laws might be socially defined or enforced.

52. **Chargaff, Erwin. Voices in the Labyrinth: Nature, Man and Science.** New York, NY: Seabury Press, 1977. 192 pages.

A noted biochemist addresses contemporary issues on the philosophy of science. Chargaff is not very optimistic about the role of science in contemporary society and warns those who would see it only as a panacea. In more recent times, Chargaff has criticized advances in genetic engineering, saying that this particular biological science could lead humanity into what he calls a "molecular Auschwitz."

53. **Chase, Alston. Playing God in Yellowstone: The Destruction of America's First National Park.** New York, NY: Atlantic Monthly, 1986. 446 pages.

The strength of this work by Alston Chase is its uncompromising attitude toward the preservation of wilderness. Under Chase's hypercritical umbrella, reform ecology, the environmental movement, even ecophilosophy, remains suspect as social and political quietisms, providing little more than quasimystical ideologies and ambivalent separatism from real environmental concerns.

With the systematic destruction of Yellowstone National Park as his critical litmus test, Chase provides a well-documented history of how our national parks, "unimpaired for future generations," are being destroyed by the very people assigned to protect and enjoy them. This paradox, claims Chase, haunts the entire ecological *Weltanschauung* of contemporary environmental philosophy and practice. As philosophical environmentalism drifts toward more theoretical issues (biocentrism, anthropocentrism, ecosophy) and larger global problems (acid rain, Green politics), it tends to leave nonhuman species to their own demise, claims Chase. While worrying about the fate of earth, species chauvinism, paradigm change, or deep, deeper, and deepest ecology, the New Philosophies of Nature risk losing touch with the very real fate of such places as Yellowstone National Park (see pages 293–368). A well-argued and well-documented work that will undoubtedly prove controversial among environmentalists and ecologists of all kinds. Extensive notes.

54. **Cheny, Jim, and Warren, Karen. Ecological Feminism and Why It Matters.** (Forthcoming).

Using sex-gender analysis, the authors show the various ways in which ecology is profoundly a feminist issue. The relationship between patriarchy and Western values is explored, as are the historical connections between the domination of nature and the domination of women. The book argues that feminist theory must include an ecological perspective, as should solutions to ecological problems include a feminist perspective. The book also critiques other versions of environmental philosophy, including deep ecology, animal rights theory, and Leopoldian land-ethics. A concluding chapter summarizes the book's most salient points, all of which lean toward a creating of an environmental ethic based on key ecofeminist principles.

55. **Clark, John. The Anarchist Moment:**
Reflections on Culture, Nature and Power.
Montreal: Black Rose Books, 1984. 250 pages.

Anarchistic thought has been linked to ecological thought on a variety of political and philosophical levels (one immediately thinks of *Earth First!* here). *The Anarchist Moment* tries to address the broader issues of anarchy from the perspective of ecological concerns and philosophies of nature. Most of the ten chapters, however, only indirectly touch upon deep ecological issues and deal primarily with the theoretical problems of classical anarchism and class structure. chapters 4, 7, 8, and 9 deal most directly with ecological concerns, offering invaluable insights into the political and social effectiveness of ecological movements—the liberating potentialities of the utopian ecological vision.

As one might suspect, Clark's book is noticeably influenced by the work of ecophilosopher Murray Bookchin. In fact, chapter 9, "The Social Ecology of Murray Bookchin" (pp. 201–228), provides one of the best critical analyses of Bookchin's work to date. In chapter 7, "Master Lao and the Anarchistic Prince" (pp. 165–199), Clark summarizes the eco–anarchistic vision of philosophical Taoism. Clark insists that the Taoism of Lao-Tzu was both anti-authoritarian and ecologically conscious. He recognizes that philosophical Taoism sought not only the end of the domination of human by the state, but also the end of the domination of nature in its realization of the path of Tao. Notes.

56. **Clark, John, ed. Renewing the Earth: The**
Promise of Social Ecology. London, England:
Marshall Pickering, 1989 (forthcoming).

Writings in honor of Murray Bookchin, whose ideas have, for the past thirty-five years, been the major inspiration for the development of social ecology, ecological (Green) politics, and alternative technology. The work is divided into three major parts: "A New Vision of the World," "A New Vision of Community," and "A New Vision of the Self." A postscript by Murray

Bookchin, "Ecologizing the Dialectic," completes the anthology, and gives the honoree's most recent thinking on the nature of self, environment, community and ethics. John Clark's introduction to the piece, "A New Philosophy for the Green Movement," places the Social Ecology Philosophy within the historical context of the worldwide Green movement and gives several reasons for social ecology's promise as a theory for regenerating both society and nature. Six of the work's seventeen essays are by John Mohawk, Morris Berman, Gary Snyder, Stephen Schecter, John Ely, and Daniel Chodorkoff. Other notable entries include poetry by Grace Paley and song lyrics by recording artist Jonathan Stevens. Contributor notes.

57. **Clark, Stephen. The Moral Status of Animals.**
Oxford, England: Clarendon Press, 1977.
221 pages.

A polemical and controversial publication, this well-documented book summarizes virtually every point of view on animal rights and morality. Clark's "consciously outrageous" publication (preface) argues that all flesh-foods and most biomedical research should be discontinued. Comprehensive in scope, the author envisions a natural order in which nonhuman sentient beings are deserving of honor, respect, and kindness. Extensive bibliography.

58. **Clark, Stephen. The Nature of the Beast: Are Animals Moral?** Oxford, England: Oxford University Press, 1983. 127 pages.

A philosophical look at the moral status of animals. Clark, as in his earlier work, argues passionately on behalf of animals, claiming they are capable of thought, self-awareness, purposive and intentional actions. Clark's major theme is that our moral systems are enormously elaborated rationalizations of pre-rational sentiments we share with other animals. A well-documented study and a necessary appendage to the animal rights literature. Comprehensive bibliography.

59. **Cobb, John, and Griffin, David. Mind in Nature: Essays on the Interface of Science and Philosophy.** Washington, D.C.: University Press of America, 1977. 148 pages.

Process studies has developed considerably since Alfred North Whitehead first began to concretize his revolutionary metaphysics some 75 years ago. More recently, Charles Hartshorne, John Cobb, Charles Birch, and others have elevated process philosophy to new and provocative areas. Moreover, a number of contemporary process philosophers and theologians have critically incorporated ecological principles into the theoretical domains of process philosophy and theology. These process philosophers/theologians are saying that the "organism" can no longer be viewed as separate from its "environment" because living entities evolve in reciprocal and highly interdependent relationships to greater organizing "wholes" and temporal "events."

This collection of papers by process thinkers is an attempt to come to terms with such a science and philosophy of "organism." Published under the auspices of the Center for Process Studies, *Mind in Nature* is divided into four parts. Part one, "The Evolution of Mind," describes the mystery of the rise of self-consciousness, mind out of nature. Part two, "Mind and Order," treats the broader questions of what is meant by order in both mind and nature; how order is related to human experience and purposeful freedom. Part three, "The Primacy of Mind," opens up and questions how the ultimate entities of the universe are to be conceived: Are physical, mental, or subjective elements in reality more fundamental than physical, material, or objective ones? Part four, "Mind and Organism," deals specifically with Whitehead's philosophy of nature; consists of five expositions on his philosophy of science, his general notions of physics and biology.

60. Cohen, Michael. The Pathless Way: John Muir and the American Wilderness. Madison, WI: University of Wisconsin Press, 1984. 408 pages.

A thorough biographical account of Muir's struggles to maintain a personal harmony with nature. Cohen critically contrasts Muir's philosophical differences with both his allies and enemies. According to Cohen, whereas Muir saw nature in terms of humanity's possible cooperation with it, most of Muir's contemporaries saw human's relationship with nature in terms of object competition and strife. Cohen concludes that Muir was much more successful as a naturalist and philosopher than as a preservationist. Politically, Muir was unable little to stop the destruction of the land he so loved. A serious scholarly study of Muir's ecological orientation. Notes.

61. Colinvaux, Paul. Why Big Fierce Animals Are Rare: An Ecologist's Perspective. Princeton, NJ: Princeton University Press, 1978. 256 pages.

Though not a philosopher, Colinvaux surveys modern ecology's central ideas from a deep understanding of the natural world and its ecosystems. Written in a clear, concise style, the book is uncluttered with references or footnotes; accordingly, the author provides the reader with a bibliographic essay; an "ecological reading list."

Colinvaux examines the rarity of big fierce animals in chapter 3 (pp. 1832), concluding that a non-Eltonian understanding of the organism as a transformer of calories, illustrates that the larger the animal, the more food and energy required to sustain it. "For flesh eaters, the largest possible supply of food calories they obtain is a fraction of the bodies of their plant-eating prey, and they must use this fraction both to make bodies and as a fuel supply. Moreover, their bodies must be the big active bodies that let them hunt for a living. If one is higher still on the food chain, an eater of a flesh-eater's flesh, one has a smaller fraction to support even bigger and fiercer bodies. Which is why large fierce animals are so astonishingly (or pleasingly) rare" (p. 27).

62. **Collingwood, R. G. The Idea of Nature.**
New York, NY: Oxford University Press, 1945.
183 pages.

A prominent British philosopher and historian of philosophy surveys the different views of nature since the PreSocratics. Divided into four major divisions: "Introduction," "Greek Cosmology," "The Renaissance View of Nature," and "The Modern View of Nature," the book begins with a substantial analytic introduction to each of the periods mentioned. While Collingwood's study of Hellenic thought remains an important and invaluable contribution to our understanding of Greek cosmology—the organismic view of nature—his general method of explication has been criticized as being overly conceptual and stilted. Collingwood often reduces the natural milieu to reified *theoria*; his ideas of nature reflect scientistic *theories* about nature, *systems* of historical beliefs. The author seldom sees nature as a participated entity of personal and meaningful experience. Notes.

63. **Commoner, Barry. The Closing Circle.** New
York, NY: Knopf Publishers, 1971. 326 pages.

An early quantitative assessment of the environmental crisis. The problems of technology, population, and economics, are considered with regards to their relationship to social and cultural organization. The text remains a popular classic among environmentalists, though tends to underplay the deeper issues associated with more profound ecological concerns, namely the ethical, religious, and political aspects of ecological thought and practice. Notes.

64. **Crosby, Alfred W. Ecological Imperialism: The
Biological Expansions of Europe, 900-1900.**
New York, NY: Cambridge University Press,
1987. 400 pages.

This evocative text represents a major first step toward the creation of a comprehensive history of the world environment. The author explores and interprets the ecological imperialism of the Europeans over the past ten centuries, concluding that the military might of the Europeans was less important than the biological strength of the plants, animals, and germs they brought with them. The widespread displacement and replacement of native peoples by Europeans, in temperate zones, argues Crosby, was due primarily to the newly introduced *organisms*; the advantages that those organisms had over their New World and Australasian counterparts. By focusing as much on the organisms as on the emigrants themselves, Crosby advances an environmental history with profound socio-political implications. Studies in Environmental History and Historical Ecology. Comprehensive bibliography and notes.

65. **Cronon, William. Changes in the Land: Indians, Colonists, and the Ecology of New England.** New York, NY: Hill and Wang, 1983. 241 pages.

Cronon's book shows how the transition from Indian to English ways of life dramatically transformed the ecology of colonial New England. Cronon contrasts the two societies in terms of their agriculture, their relationship to animals, their differently held notions of property, their varying degrees of respect for the land. Unlike most historians who document the social and cultural transformations of a particular time or place, this author emphasizes the *environmental* impact of the colonial settlements in the New World. This fact makes Cronon's book of particular importance to ecologists: the author insists that the relationship of the two groups to their environment possesses a tremendous historical importance in understanding the entire history of a region and its peoples.

The text is divided into three parts: Part one consisting of a single introductory chapter, "The View from Walden" (pp. 315). Part two, which is by far the largest portion of the work, outlines the ecological transformation of colonial New England in its entirety. Part three, a single concluding chapter, "That Wilderness Should Turn a Mart" (pp. 159–70), critiques the capitalistic tendencies of the early colonial settlers; their overt concern with international markets and trade. Extensive notes. Ends with a "Bibliographic Essay" of over 500 entries. Environmental and regional history.

66. **Davis, Gregory H. Technology—Humanism or Nihilism: A Critical Analysis of the Philosophical Basis and Practice of Modern Technology.** Washington, D.C.: University Presses of America, 1981. 278 pages.

Throughout this text, Davis warns of the dangerous nihilistic and dehumanizing effects of technology, the ability of technology to transform every aspect of human life. Accordingly, he argues for a technology designed to give humans more control over their own lives—technologies that are contained in, or restrained by, human cultural values. Notes.

67. **Day, David. The Doomsday Book of Animals: A Natural History of Vanished Species.** New York, NY: Viking Press, 1981. 287 pages.

A beautifully illustrated reference work that chronicles the extinction of the world's animal species, *The Doomsday Book of Animals* is also an excellent and well-documented "read." Divided into three parts, "Birds," "Mammals," and "Reptiles, Amphibians, and Fish," each chapter and each entry is a self-contained narrative describing the known history of each vanished animal species. The appendix glosses over the extinction of most vascular plant species and contains a helpful world atlas of all known extinct animal varieties. Also supplies the reader with an index listing the taxonomic order of all vanished and severely endangered animals.

68. **Debus, Allen G. Man and Nature in the Renaissance.** Cambridge, MA: Cambridge University Press, 1978. 159 pages.

As Debus himself notes in this volume, the medieval knowledge of flora and fauna derived in a large part from Pliny the Elder's *Natural History*, written in the first century A.D. The study of nature in the Middle Ages did, in general, owe a great deal to the writings of the ancients. However, as Debus ably demonstrates in this small volume, the Renaissance image of nature began to slowly change—began to alter not only the study of nature, but our relationship to it as well.

Throughout the text, the author provides a methodical outline of the subtle evolutions in science, technology, and nature philosophy during roughly the period between 1450 to 1750. The leading thinkers and ideas of the period are discussed either singly or in the context of changing scientific attitudes of the period. Debus does well to keep his discussions in the context of *natural* history; he avoids being overly humanistic in his approach. Overall, the book provides a well-documented, well-reasoned study of the origins of our modern understanding of science and nature. Includes also an extensive suggested reading list of over two hundred entries, categorized by topic.

69. **Deloria, Vine, Jr. The Metaphysics of Modern Existence.** San Francisco, CA: Harper & Row, 1979. 233 pages.

In this impressive synthesis of a number of trains of thought, Vine Deloria, the author of *God Is Red* (1973), describes a worldview that bridges science and religion, knowledge and meaning. The metaphysics of modern existence, argues Deloria, is hopelessly reductionistic, ethnocentric, out of touch with nature. The primitive worldview, on the other hand, is not only ecologically superior, but is also epistemologically defendable as an equally veridical way of experiencing reality. The Western notion of knowledge divorces knowing from experience, the primitive confronts existence not as something that is to be understood in the epistemological sense, but as something that is *participated*. The primitive mind incorporates all aspects of experience into his systems of belief, providing the person with a felt concrete reference to the existential unity of the natural and social world(s). Includes an appendix of what Deloria calls "the emerging dissident literature" (literature rejecting the assumptions of Western science and philosophy).

70. **Derrick, C. The Delicate Creation: Towards a Theology of the Environment.** Old Greenwich, CT: Devin-Adair, 1972. 129 pages.

A theology of the environment based primarily on Catholic principles. Foreword by René Dubos; introduction by John Cardinal Wright.

71. **Detweiler, Robert; Sutherland, John; and Werthman, Michael, eds. Environmental Decay in Its Historical Context.** Glenview, IL: Scott, Foresman, and Company, 1973. 142 pages.

This anthology, by a variety of authors, is comprised of both well- and little-known essays on the environmental decay of Western civilization. On the more familiar side, there are essays by John Storer, Lynn White, Jr., Paul Ehrlich, Barry Commoner, Rachel Carson, Clarence Glacken, Lewis Mumford, and René Dubos—all of which have appeared in earlier printed sources. On the less familiar side, there are essays by Marc Bloch, "Medieval Land Clearance" (pp. 7577), and Jerome Carcopino, "Living Conditions in Ancient Rome" (pp. 9092). Although all 27 essays were originally published prior to 1971—and have a particular dated quality—when viewed together they provide the reader with a good overview of the historical and cultural prerequisites generally associated with environmental degradation. The text is arranged in five sections, each prefaced with a brief essay by the editors. Historical and Human Ecology.

72. **Devall, Bill. Simple in Means, Rich in Ends: Practicing Deep Ecology.** Layton, UT: Gibbs M. Smith, 1988 (in press).

A forthcoming statement, on the practice of deep ecology, by one of the founders of the deep ecology movement.

73. **Devall, Bill, and Sessions, George. Deep Ecology: Living as if Nature Mattered.**

Salt Lake City, UT: Peregrine Smith Books,
1985. 266 pages.

Deep ecology, a neologism coined by Norwegian philosopher and environmentalist Arne Naess, refers to the process of asking deeper, more profound questions about the nature of Nature, consciousness, and culture. The book *Deep Ecology*, written by Bill Devall, a sociologist, and George Sessions, a professor of philosophy, tells the reader that contemporary ecophilosophical thought is critically engaged in (1) cultivating an "ecological consciousness"; (2) exploring the anthropological, sociological, psychological, and philosophical roots of our modern industrial civilization; (3) addressing the moral, axiological, and critical aporias of a society living uncontemporaneously with the natural processes; and (4) critiquing the arrogant anthropocentricism of contemporary scholarship/practice. For example, the authors argue in this work—borrowing words from philosopher Pete Gunter—that "pragmatism, Marxism, scientific humanism, French positivism, German mechanism . . . the whole swarm of smug anti-religious dogmas . . . now deeply entrenched in scientific, political, economic, and educational institutions really do not, as they claim, make man a part of nature. If anything, they make nature an extension of and mere raw material for man" (p. 54).

For those familiar with the more mundane methodologies of "text book" ecology, the preceding statement may seem curiously out of character. Traditionally, the academy has not seen the ecological worldview as laying the groundwork for a socially relevant critique of our present era. Fostering a practice guided by a rigorous theory in both the broadest and deepest sense, ecological philosophy, as Paul Shepherd states in the introduction to the book *The Subversive Science* (1969), attempts to deconstruct *all* the dominant Western views of man. Anyone even vaguely familiar with ecophilosophical principles should, therfore, regard ecological thought as a necessary appendage to the critical literature.

The deep ecology philosophy, itself an integral part of the ecophilosophical project, is an original and ambitious attempt to lay the foundations of such a critical ecology (however porous and inconsistent its foundational bedrock sometimes appears). Future attempts at fleshing out deep ecology's fundamental principles will undoubtedly strenghten its present theoretical weaknesses. While present studies have dealt more rigorously with the human/nature problematic, *Deep Ecology* will undoubtedly remain an important introduction to the deep ecology literature. Substantial appendixes in this work by Arne Naess, Carolyn Merchant, Robert Roshi, George Sessions, John Seed, Dolores LaChapelle, and Gary Snyder. Annotated bibliography, notes.

74. **Diamond, Stanley. In Search of the Primitive:**
    A Critique of Civilization. New Brunswick,
    NJ: Transaction Books, 1974. 387 pages.

    A provocative critique of anthropology as it is commonly practiced in academia. Diamond, a former professor of anthropology in the graduate faculty of the New School of Social Research, critically re-examines our present understanding of primitive cultures and traditions. In chapter 1, "Civilization and Progress" (pp. 148), Diamond critiques the progressive and imperialistic cultures that give birth to such inauthentic disciplines as "cultural anthropology." In chapter 2, "The Politics of Field Work" (pp. 49–92), the author rejects the methodologies of state-financed anthropology and their repressive ideologies and condescending ethnocentrisms. After questioning the possible role of anthropology in an emancipatory study of man, Diamond begins his search for the primitive in the book's title chapter (pp. 116–175). "In Search of the Primitive" is an evocative essay on the existential dynamics of primitive life. The author finds the primitive mode of being as largely a healthy and positive one—in harmony with nature—conducive to the enrichment of individual and social experience. Critical and Philosophical Anthropology. Notes.

75. **Dinnerstein, Dorothy. The Mermaid and the**
    Minotaur: Sexual Arrangements and the
    Human Malaise. New York, NY: Harper &
    Row, 1976. 288 pages.

    The study in question is an exploration of the psychosexual roots of human oppression and the domination of nature. Dinnerstein critiques the sexual arrangements and child-rearing practices of contemporary Western culture as well as the relationships to science and technology they facilitate. It is the "megamachine" of the patriarchal sensibility, says the author, that allows for the cultural replacement of the "gifts of nature" with the social controls of hierarchical rule and submission. A more matricentric understanding of the human condition is needed in order to resurrect the organic sensibilities of life-enhancing social arrangements, concludes the author. Ecofeminism.

76. **Dodson Gray, Elizabeth. Green Paradise Lost.**
    Wellesley, MA: Roundtable Press, 1982.
    166 pages.

    Ecophilosophy has often acknowledged the relationship between ecological and feminist values: the psycho-sexual roots of the ecological crisis has always been an important concern of ecophilosophical literature. *Green Paradise Lost* summarizes the ecofeminist vision presently embraced by many ecophilosophers, critiquing our religious and cultural heritage as both paternally hierarchical and politically oppressive. Gray insists that we need to "re-myth" our place in nature as well as rediscover the intricate connections between consciousness and creation. Ecology, for Gray, is a way of seeing the world anew, an embodied dynamic that seeks the end of hierarchical views of reality. The thesis: An ecofeminist epistemology should provide the necessary impetus for sustained ecological change as well as a non-hierarchical concept of human identity. Notes.

77. Drengson, Alan R. Shifting Paradigms: From Technocrat to Planetary Person. Lightstar Press, P.O. Box 5853, Stn. B, Victoria, B.C. V8R–6S8, 1983. 166 pages.

A noted ecophilosopher studies the emerging paradigm shifts in Western consciousness and philosophy. Drengson sets forth and catalogs the existential prerequisites for such paradigm shifts, ultimately arguing that the mechanistic worldview of the technocrat is rapidly giving way to an ecological consciousness of revolutionary proportions. According to the author, the new ecological paradigm will capture and sustain the values of ecological belief systems. Community, interrelationship, respect for all living things, species integrity, planetary consciousness, and social responsibility will be the values embraced by the "pernetarian" (planetary person) culture. A good overview of the major philosophical tenets in ecophilosophical literature. Appendixes. Extensive bibliography.

78. Drengson, Alan R. Beyond Environmental Crisis: From Technocrat to Planetary Person. New York: Peter Lang, 1989 (in press).

A substantially revised edition of the author's earlier work, *Shifting Paradigms* (1983). Focuses on the way ecological philosophizing may be raised to the level of art, or applied creative activity. The author believes that structuring an environmental ethic without analyzing the deeper structures of modern Western consciousness has, in an ecological sense, many inherent limitations. With entirely new materials, Drengson offers a philosophical approach that is powerful enough in Western society "to clarify the ecological sense and dimensions of the relationships between community, self and Nature." An epilogue, "Ecosophy and the Way," gives concrete examples of how we can proceed toward ecosophical alternatives in our daily lives and practices. Notes. Appendixes.

79. Dryzek, John. Rational Ecology: The Political Economy of Environmental Choice. London, England: Basil Blackwell (forthcoming).

80. **Dubos, René. A God Within.** New York, NY: Charles Scribner's Sons, 1972. 326 pages.

A Pulitzer Prize winning scientist expounds on an ecological "theology of the earth." Although most chapters do not deal as overtly with deep theological issues as suggested, there are a few chapters that attempt to do so. In chapter 8, for example, "Franciscan Conservation Versus Benedictine Conservation" (pp. 153–74), Dubos critiques the conservation ethic of Franciscan theology, taking sides with the more humanistic Benedictine approach. "Because of my own cultural tradition," writes the author, "I have chosen to (favorably) illustrate . . . the Benedictine way of life—its wisdom in managing the land, in fitting architecture to worship and landscape, in adapting rituals and work to the cosmic rhythms" (p. 174). A thoroughly humanized ecology of nature.

81. **Dubos, René. The Wooing of Earth.** New York, NY: Charles Scribner's Sons, 1980. 183 pages.

According to the author, in a creative and balanced understanding of the relationship of humanity and nature is an awareness that the environment is "improvable" to some degree by human intervention,i.e., the successful intervention of nature by humanity *requires* a process of improving upon nature in what is called the "humanization of the earth" (chapter 5, pp. 49–78). It is only this "wooing of earth," says Dubos, that makes one aware of the spiritual and visceral values linking humanity to the biosphere.

The author argues that the creative embellishment of nature by man creates the most desirable ecological conditions for the respect, rather than the domination, of our natural environment. He insists that his position does not take human beings out of the natural order, nor above it. In a similar vein, he defends Judeo-Christian thought as being neither anti-ecological or overtly human-centered, summarizing a vast amount of literature on the subject (Appendix III), concluding that historically the Judeo-Christian tradition has been no more or less ecological than any other. The problem is not one of anthropocentrism, says Dubos, but one of promoting an ecological awareness that preserves man's best capabilities and at the same time preserves the best in nature. Appendixes. Notes.

82. **Ehrenfeld, David. The Arrogance of Humanism.** New York, NY: Oxford University Press, 1978. 286 pages.

A critical view of contemporary humanism, which, in Ehrenfeld's opinion, is an environmentally destructive force, practiced almost universally as religion—"the dominant religion of our time" (p. 3). Ehrenfeld's study is a thorough analysis of the assumptions of current humanistic philosophies as well as their relationship to nature and social reality. In chapter 5, for example, "The Conservation Dilemma" (pp. 176–211), Ehrenfeld effectively shows how environmentalists have generally not been able to escape the trap of humanism. Most environmentalists, argues Ehrenfeld, see nature only in terms of economic and monetary values. Fortunately, Ehrenfeld's attempt to go beyond the shortsightedness of humanism does not end with simply another anti-humanist, misanthropic polemic. In chapter 6, "Misanthropy and the Rejection of Humanism" (pp. 214–232), for example, Ehrenfeld considers whether it is even possible to totally reject humanistic visions of reality, further qualifying his position as an ecological/humanistic one. An important contribution to environmental and ecophilosophical thought. Notes.

83. **Ehrenreich, Barbara, and English, Deidre.**
For Her Own Good: 150 Years of the Experts'
Advice to Women. New York, NY: Anchor
Press/Doubleday, 1978. 325 pages.

The title of this book fails to do justice to its content. *For Her Own Good* is a well-argued, well-documented exegesis on the rise of patriarchal authority, the political suppression of matricentric attitudes over the past 150 years. What makes this book essential for ecologists is that it relates the matricentric attitude to the virtues of natural living and communal organization; the organic sensibility in general. It is only with the rise of the male expert—the doctor, lawyer, scientist, politician—that one begins to see the power/knowledge dialectic of an increasingly hierarchical society erode the ecological fabric of rural craft and custom; traditions of self-reliance. The patriarchal mentality of modern health care, unchecked urbanization, and centralized industry, maintains the authors, is a mentality incorrectly "sold" to the masses as superior. Conversely, all other sensibilities are considered pathological by those in power—condemned as heresy, witchcraft, or charlatanry.

84. **Ehrlich, Paul and Anne. Extinction:**
The Causes and Consequences of the
Disappearance of Species. New York, NY:
Ballantine, 1981. 384 pages.

The rate of species depletion is reaching unprecedented rates in human history—this fact is well publicized by the media and remains one of the most fundamental concerns of ecologists and environmentalists. Paul and Anne Ehrlich capably address the issues surrounding species extinction, concluding that the causes and consequences of the disappearances of species are questions that require not only "ecological" solutions, but political, esthetic, and ethical ones as well.

The Ehrlichs, in chapter 3, "Compassion, Esthetics, Fascination, and Ethics," outline their basic ethical position on the extinction question. They borrow heavily from the ideas of David Ehrenfeld, arguing that species and their communities should be preserved not only because they are themselves an expression of a continual historical and evolutionary process, but because they have inherent "intrinsic value." This rationale for conservation, the "Noah principle," is then projected into a "life-boat" model of the ecosphere, or what the authors have metaphorically labeled "Spaceship Earth." According to the authors, "Spaceship Earth" represents the planet we live on, the ecological web that constructs the global ecology, the nurturing vessel that sustains all life. In the reviewer's opinion, the reduction of the living biotic community to the machinations of sci-fi metaphors, however convenient, suggests a rather oversimplification of the preservation problem. Not only does this technocentric imagery uncritically retain the "resource utilitarianism" it ultimately wants to condemn, it also reduces intrinsic value to cost-efficient economic benefits. (See, for example, chapter 4, "Direct Economic Benefits of Preserving Species" (pp. 63–90) and chapter 5, "Indirect Benefits: Life Support Systems" (pp. 91–120).)

Despite these deficiencies, *Extinction* remains an important work, empirically documenting the rate of species loss, warning of the social and environmental consequences of the elimination of the world's plant and animal life. Includes an Appendix: "Taxonomy of Organisms Discussed." Notes.

85. **Eiseley, Loren C. The Invisible Pyramid.** New York, NY: Scribner and Sons, 1970. 173 pages.

Philosophical essays by an eminent American anthropologist. Eiseley, the author of *The Immense Journey* (1957) and *The Firmament of Time* (1960), examines the nature of humanity in the modern industrial world. The author perceptively contrasts the aspirations of ancient civilization with modern ones, pointing out the specific differences in their relationships to the natural world. Eiseley argues that modern man, like his ancient predecessors, must develop an empathetic relationship with other creatures. A classic ecophilosophical work.

86. **Elder, Frederick. Crisis in Eden: A Religious Study of Man and Environment.** Nashville, TN: Abingdon Press, 1970. 173 pages.

Elder suggests that the environmental crisis can be resolved by advancing a holistic theological approach to humanity's position in the natural order. This approach, claims Elder, would embrace an activist asceticism emphasizing voluntary restraint, the quality of existence, and the reverence for all life. Extensive bibliography. Christian stewardship.

87. **Elgin, Duane. Voluntary Simplicity: An Ecological Lifestyle that Promotes Personal**

and Social Renewal. New York, NY: Bantam Books, 1982. 264 pages.

Voluntary simplicity is about choosing simpler, more ecologically aware lifestyles. The author sees the ecological consciousness as a less destructive, more rewarding way of life. But because the author also sees the ecological consciousness as a corollary to human consciousness, one cannot have respect for the earth without having respect for other people. Voluntary simplicity is neither a separatist nor misanthropic worldview. In the first chapter, Elgin defines the political, psychological, and religious characteristics of voluntary simplicity; its historical roots and common heritage with related attitudes. The book closes with a comparison of the voluntary simplicity idea with Eastern traditions, as well as ways of integrating the two approaches. Appendixes, including a substantial suggested reading list (Appendix One). Introduction by Ram Dass.

88. **Eliade, Mircea. The Myth of the Eternal Return.** Princeton, NJ: Princeton University Press, 1954. 195 pages.

A noted historian of religion, in a book of great insight and scholarship, studies the sacred aspects of primitive ritual; their profound existential relationship to cycles in nature, cosmic time, and regenerative mythology. Comparative anthropology.

89. **Elliot, Robert, and Gare, Arran. Environmental Philosophy: A Collection of Readings.** St. Lucia, Queensland and New York: University of Queensland Press, 1983. 303 pages.

A collection of twelve essays by leading ecophilosophers on a variety of topical issues, *Environmental Philosophy* is divided into three parts: "Environmental Policy and Human Welfare," "A New Environmental Ethic?" and "Attitudes in the Natural Environment." There are essays (to name but five of the authors represented) by Holmes Rolston, III, Mary Anne Warren, Mary Midgeley, J. Baird Callicot, and Richard Routley. One of the more reappearing concerns in this anthology is the problem of intrinsic values in nature. The question is left somewhat unresolved, however, as each thinker confronts the issue from noticeably different perspectives. Though the essays in this volume do represent a mixed-bag of philosophical positions, the book remains an important addition to the environmental philosophy literature.

90. **Ellul, Jacques. The Technological Society.** Translated by John Wilkinson. New York, NY: Vintage Books, 1964. 449 pages.

French sociologist Jacques Ellul, one of the most renowned critics of modern technology and culture, provides a penetrating analysis of our technical civilization, the social and psychological effects of an increasingly standardized social order. According to Ellul, "History shows that every technical application from its beginning presents unforeseeable secondary effects which are more disastrous than the lack of the technique would have been" (p. 105). The high degree at which the author says technique dominates society and consciousness has been criticized, however, by those who see technique as a much less deterministic factor in defining and controlling human consciousness. Whatever Ellul's philosophical deficiencies, *The Technological Society*, as Robert Merton notes in his introduction to the text, "requires us to examine anew . . . the essential tragedy of a civilization increasingly dominated by technique" (p. v). Notes.

91. **Elton, C. S. The Ecology of Invasions by Animals and Plants.** London, England: Methuen, 1958. 181 pages.

An important and original study of plant and animal "invasions"; the behavior and ecology of species' populations in new or unnatural environments. A prominent British ecologist, Elton observes the evolution of a number of species in both Old and New World settings. Elton's views on conservation are highly advanced for his generation of ecologists, see particularly chapters 8 and 9: "The Reasons for Conservation" (pp. 143–153), "The Conservation of Reality" (pp. 154–159). Historical ecology, illustrations.

92. **Engel, J. Ronald. Sacred Sands: The Struggle for Community in the Indiana Dunes.** Middletown, CT: Wesleyan University Press, 1983. 352 pages.

Engel, in describing and interpreting the struggles to preserve the "sacred sands" of the Indiana Dunes, documents the social, cultural, and religious aspects that came together to save this region and establish the Indiana Dunes National Lakeshore in 1966. The author rightly reminds us that the campaign for preservation must involve a far deeper and more complex set of emotions than those ordinarily prescribed by lay ecologists. Accordingly, *Sacred Sands* deals with the ecological awareness of such visionaries as Donald C. Peattie, Edwin Teale, Earl Howell Reed, Sr., and the artists, writers, reformers, and activists who joined together in the struggle to save this unique landscape. Maps, illustrations, notes.

93. **Evernden, Neil. The Natural Alien: Humankind and Environment.** Toronto: University of Toronto Press, 1985. 160 pages.

Evernden, a professor of environmental studies at York University, draws mostly from phenomenology in his thoughtful attempt to distill the "*a priori* essences from nature." In this quasi-Husserlian, quasi-Merleau-Pontian plea to return to the "things themselves," Evernden claims that modern industrial man is a "natural alien." The human species, says the author, is presently rootless, homeless—estranged from the natural environment. The author is obviously familiar with the most recent literature in the ecophilosophy field. His reappraisal of the environmental movement reflects an informed sensitivity to the philosophical issues involved.

The text is divided into four areas, each area discussing the resistance of Western society in considering the concept of self as being integrated in nature's processes. Chapter 3, "Returning to Experience" (pp. 55–72), outlines the phenomenological project of returning to the primacy of experience, the basic epistemological positions of Husserl and Heidegger—their championing of a "being" that embodies the totality of human experience. For Evernden, foundational ecology, in the name of "environmental ethics," fails to appreciate the possibility of a new awareness of being, an *ethos* that could radically alter our understanding of ourselves and our world. "In a society dominated by the technological vision," writes Evernden, "there is no possibility of an environmental ethic" (p. 69). To regain the natural attitude, he argues, we must rediscover our world anew. Other noteworthy chapters include "A Biology of Subjects" (pp. 73–102) and the "Shells of Belief" (pp. 125–44), a summary of the present philosophical and cultural attitudes surrounding environmentalism and ecology (pp. 125–144). Extensive notes.

94. Flader, Susan L. Thinking Like a Mountain:
Aldo Leopold and the Evolution of an
Ecological Attitude toward Deer, Wolves,
and Forests. Columbia, MO: The University
of Missouri Press, 1974. 284 pages.

In this volume, Flader examines the ways in which the author of *A Sand County Almanac* (1949) formed his attitudes toward wildlife, wilderness, and appropriate land use. Aldo Leopold's thinking has been an enormous influence on today's environmental philosophy literature. The scholarship of this volume makes an important contribution to the study of Leopold's ecological policies and observations. The work also documents, in detail, the travels of Leopold, the many writings borne of those same travels.

In chapter 4, "Means and Ends: The 1930s," Flader describes Leopold's visit to Germany's "slick-and-clean" spruce forest in 1935. Leopold was apparently appalled by the artificiality of the forest and game management he observed there. The Germans had in essence created "tree-factories" of long rotated, high-yield timber crops which created foodless areas for hundreds of animal species, including deer. Consequently, in order to maintain high-intensity deer populations, the deer had to be fed and ranged artificially, which, in turn, created even greater shortages of food not only for the deer, but for the other forest animals that required those same foods. Leopold sadly concluded that the objectives of forest and game management—to maintain the integrity of the diverse biotic community—"were being undermined by the very techniques of the environmental control used to obtain them" (p. 143). The paradox of this utilitarian conservation ethic and practice, says Flader, was to play an important role in shaping Leopold's future environmental policies and prejudices in America. Americans, argued Leopold, must preserve not only aesthetic values in nature, they must also concentrate on preserving the integrity of the *entire* land community. Biographical Notes.

95. Foreman, David, and Haywood, Dave, eds.
     Ecodefense: A Field Guide to
     Monkeywrenching. 2nd ed. Tucson, AZ:
     Earth First! Books, 1987. 312 pages.

A manual for eco-anarchists, eco-saboteurs and the like. Inspired by Edward Abbey's novel *The Monkey Wrench Gang* (1975), monkey-wrenching has become an important (and perhaps neccessary) pastime for environmental reactionaries. *Ecodefense* should, therefore, be of use to only the most radical of ecophilosophers. This revised and substantially larger edition gives information about "tree-spiking," removing billboards, fence cutting, etc. The editors are founding members of *Earth First!*—the organization whose motto is: "no compromise in the defense of mother earth!" Forward! by Edward Abbey.

96. Foster, Charles. Experiments in
     Bioregionalism: The New England River
     Basin Story. Hanover, NH: University Press
     of New England, 1984. 240 pages.

The author has been commissioner of the Massachusetts Departments of Natural Resources, president of the Nature Conservancy, and dean of the Yale School of Forestry and Environmental Studies. His study comes from a deep understanding of New England, its regional personality, its cultural traditions and natural boundaries. The work is well documented and carefully researched, but remains more of a governmental than populist formulation of the bioregionalist concept. This book, in sum, addresses the issues of scale; the role of critical mass and political function in maintaining the bioregional consciousness of the New England river basin.

97. Fox, Michael. Returning to Eden: Animal
     Rights and Human Responsibility. New
     York, NY: Viking Press, 1980. 281 pages.

In the introduction to this exegesis on animal rights and human responsibility, Michael Fox, the executive director of the Humane Society, notes: "Human valuation is wholly dependent upon the liberation of nature from our selfish treatment and on humane consideration. Human liberation will begin when we understand that our evolution and fulfillment are contingent on the recognition of animal rights and on a compassionate and responsible stewardship of nature" (p. xiv). Appropriately, the remaining pages of *Returning to Eden* address the need to acknowledge the unity of human existence with all other lifeforms. Subsequent chapters discuss the biological and cultural relationship between humans and nature, the uses and abuses of animals, science and nature, the religious and moral aspects of protecting animals and animal species. For those seeking specific information about Animal Welfare Laws and Federal Agencies dealing with animal protection, a valuable resource list is appended. Suggested reading list.

98. **Fox, Warwick. Approaching Deep Ecology: A Response to Richard Sylvan's Critique of Deep Ecology.** University of Tasmania, Hobart, Australia, Environmental Studies Occasional Paper 20, 1986. 116 pages.

In a well-known paper entitled, "A Critique of Deep Ecology," Richard Sylvan has argued (in so many words) that deep ecology is primarily a conceptual theory, a system of beliefs based on a doctrine of values drawn inaccurately from nature. In this lengthy response to Sylvan's unsympathetic diatribe, Fox, an Australian ecophilosopher, methodically defends deep ecology's metaphysical and practical positions.

The author adroitly argues that the axiological and ontological principles of deep ecology are irreducible to the traditional theoretical and analytical tenets ascribed to it by Sylvan. Deep ecology, insists Fox, is much more than an analytical interpretation of the human/nature relationship. In the deep ecology axiology, for example, values are not derived solely from the intrinsic quality of things in nature (as Sylvan suggests), but from the quality of the *relationship* between a thing in nature and the self. The self of deep ecology—the "ecological consciousness"—experiences the world as valuable in the *process* of identification with the whole of nature. Deep ecology, claims Fox, is not so much interested with whether the nonhuman world is good enough for us (intrinsically valuable) as whether we are able to sustain the greatest possible identification with the whole of nature. A major (albeit conversationally polemical) discussion on the principles of deep ecology. Notes.

99. **Fritsch, Albert J. Renew the Face of the Earth.** Chicago, Illinois, IL: Loyola University Press, 1987. 280 pages.

The author is the current director of *Appalachia–Science in the Public Interest*, as well as the author of several books related to ecophilosophical themes (see, for example, his *Appalachia: A Meditation*, 1986). In this, his most recent work, Fritsch gives us a completely Christianized philosophy of nature, using a creative and ecumenical blend of scriptural, liturgical, and theological sources. Fritsch argues that Christanity must have a firm foundation in environmentalism if it is to authentically "partake in the glory of God's Creation." Love and respect for the things of the earth, says the author, is a necessity within the Judeo-Christian tradition.

In chapter 4, "Ascension: An Invitation to Environmental Educators" (pp. 97–130), Fritsch turns to the responsibility of stewardship to environmental instructors, who, in his view, must also view creation in its most sacred, unifying forms. This point is reiterated in later discussions where the question of environmental ecumenism is addressed—"The environmental movement," says Fritsch, "is divided in various factions (public interest laywers, alternative lifestyle people, radical activists, educators, etc.). Some groups disregard the efforts of other members of the movement and overemphasize their own activities. The struggle for unity among the Christian communities has resulted in a learned experience which is useful within the environmental movement. If ecology is inherent in Christianity, then unity among 'greens' is found germinally within the movement toward Christian unity. Forms of Christian celebration may offer the means of holding the emerging environmental community together" (pp. 209–210). Notes and appendix.

100. **Glacken, Clarence. Traces on the Rhodian Shore: Nature and Culture in Western Thought from Ancient Times to the End of the Eighteenth Century.** Berkeley, CA: University of California Press, 1967. 763 pages.

The author presents parallel histories from classical times to the end of the eighteenth century on three related themes: the idea of the earth as created by design, the influence of environment on man, and the influence of man on the environment. More specifically, the book presents a broad history of cosmological ideas, articulated through a highly interdisciplinary framework—geographer Glacken relates social and natural phenomena to the dichotomy perennially occurring between man and nature. Glacken uses original sources frequently and with scholarly attention—an extraordinary synthesis of a vast literature of Western thought. Historical ecology, nature cosmology. Bibliography and notes.

101. **Goodpaster, K. E., and Sayre, K. M., eds. Ethics and the Problems of the 21st Century.**

Notre Dame, IN: The University of Notre
Dame Press, 1979. 207 pages.

With support from the National Science Foundation, the editors have collected and arranged a number of original essays on the application of ethical theory to ecological issues and concerns. Essays by W. K. Frankena, R. and V. Routley, Kenneth Goodpaster, R. M. Hare, Jonathan Glover, Peter Singer and others. The papers are organized under three normative areas: concepts of morality (Frankena, Goodpaster, the Routleys), methods and principles of moral reflection (Hare, J. Glover, R. T. DeGeorge, R. Coburn, and A. MacIntyre), and the application of normative principles to concrete, substantive issues (A. Gewirth, K. Baier, N. Goldig, Singer). All of those in the first section would extend morality to include nonhuman. In the second section all but MacIntyre agree to some sort of normative methodology. The remaining essays discuss a variety of issues, the right of starving people to be given food, the sanctity of life, landmark preservation, and animal rights.

102. **Gorz, André. Ecology as Politics.** Boston, MA:
South End Press, 1980. 215 pages.

A perfunctory neo-Marxian analysis of ecological social movements by a French social theorist. Gorz's notion of ecology does, however, sometimes present itself as a rather shallow environmentalist one, overtly and reductively painting ecology in mostly economic and political terms. Rather than illustrating how an ecological sensibility might *yield* a particular political orientation or economic base, Gorz simply discusses ecology's *impact* on existing modes of social organization. Unfortunately, Gorz's solution to current environmental problems relies heavily on the "self-management" techniques of neo-Marxian thought. An intellectual pastiche of ecological ideas.

103. **Graber, Linda H. Wilderness as Sacred Space.**
Washington, D.C.: Association of American
Geographers, 1976. 124 pages.

A monograph uniting religious, philosophical, sociological, political, aesthetic, and literary materials. The author, a humanistic geographer, argues that proponents of wilderness areas are, in part, motivated by their religious experience of wilderness as sacred space. Graber's treatment of religious experience is more of an aesthetic than institutional religious one, however; in her eyes we experience wilderness phenomenologically, as an epiphanic "wholly other." Overall, a purely descriptive, ahistorical reading of the sacred wilderness experience.

104. **Granberg-Michaelson, Wesley. A Worldly
Spirituality: The Call to Redeem Life on**

Earth. New York, NY: Harper & Row, 1984.
210 pages.

A spiritual call for a caring, nurturing relationship with the whole of God's creation—a new "Christian theology of the earth." Divided into three parts: (1) "The Peril: Creation Destroyed," (2) "The Promise: Creation Redeemed," and (3) "The Prospect: Creation Restored," *A Worldly Spirituality* critically intergrates sociological, political, and economic thought with biblical, theological, and ethical teachings.

Granberg-Michaelson's arguments rest mostly on the doctrine of Creationism—*the earth is the Lord's and the fullness thereof.* However, the author, a member of the Community Covenant Church in Missoula, Montana, introduces additional theological and spiritual doctrine into this holistic ecological theology; namely, the gift of grace and Christian charity—"The beauty and radiance of the creation resides not simply in itself, but rather in its relationship to God. Here is where Christianity distinguishes itself from various froms of animism and pantheism. All life in creation exists only because of God. Its glory and majesty is simply the occasion for creation to reflect grace back to God. Just as a person becomes lovely in God's eyes as he or she receives God's grace, so all creation is being transformed through the radiance of God's grace" (p. 132). Concludes with an informed critique of biotechnology, "Authoring Life" (pp. 187–196). Foreword by Jeremy Rifkin. Postscript. Notes and substantial bibliography.

105. **Grant, George. Technology and Justice.** Notre
Dame, IN: University of Notre Dame Press,
1986. 133 pages.

In George Grant's words, "technology is the ontology of the age" (p.32). Technology has imperialized Western being and becoming to the extent that it has "turned" on humanity, legislating not only the manner in which we live and work but also the manner in which we think, feel, and create values. In this highly relevant work, Grant, one of North America's leading political philosophers, and author of *Technology and Empire* (1969), has given us six new essays on the impact of technology on modern life and values. Essays include discussions on technology, computers, abortion, and euthanasia. Notes.

106. **Grassé, Pierre-P. Evolution of Living
Organisms: Evidence for a New Theory of
Transformation.** New York, NY: Academic
Press, 1977. 297 pages.

A provocative critique of the neo-Darwinian view of evolutionary change. Grassé, one of France's leading biologists and editor of *Le Traité de Zoologie*

(1948), brings important credentials to the task of debunking widely accepted views on developmental or "progressive" species adaptation.

107. **Griffin, Donald. Animal Thinking.**
Cambridge, MA: Harvard University Press,
1984. 237 pages.

A readable and mature statement on the question surrounding animal awareness. Griffin, a cognitive ethologist, uncovers the theoretical evidence that would suggest that animals are capable of thought, communication, and subjective feeling. Admitting that the evidence for animal thought is controversial, Griffin does not agree that it is unverifiable. Philosophically speaking, many of Griffin's assertions (attributing linguistic behavior to animals, for example) are noticeably anthropocentric, though certainly forgivable in light of new evidence for the existence of animal communication. *Animal Thinking* should remain an important stimulus for thought for future studies in this area.

108. **Griffin, Susan. Woman and Nature: The Roaring Inside Her.** San Francisco, CA: Harper & Row, 1978. 263 pages.

An unconventional and emotion-filled book. Griffin's poetic style attempts to say the unsayable by way of verse, prose, and creative dialogue. She consistently argues that women speak—in their embodiment—with and through nature. Corporeality is important, says the author, because we can know the earth only by the roaring inside us, or, in the author's words, by "the music of celestial spheres." A dialogue for/of/from the human body—nature's body. Extensive notes and bibliography. Ecofeminism.

109. **Hall, Edward T. The Dance of Life: The Other Dimension of Time.** New York, NY: Anchor Press/Doubleday, 1983. 231 pages.

Generally, ecologists have ignored the complex temporal relationships occurring between humans and other humans, humans and their natural environments. Spatial metaphors dominate the ecology lexique. For anthropologist Edward Hall, time speaks the true language of ecology—is an organizer of social and cultural activities, a synthesizer and integrator of human feelings. "Time," exclaims the author, "not only has everything to do with how a culture develops, but also with how the people of that culture experience the world" (p. 5).

Divided into two parts, "Time as Culture" and "Time as Experience," *The Dance of Life* begins with a prefatory discussion on the many varieties of social and psychological time. Subsequent chapters contain comparative analyses of Eastern and Western concepts of time (chapter 6), the time perspectives of European and American cultures (chapter 7). Part two (chapters 8-11) deals primarily with the psychology of time. Chapter 10, for example, offers a fascinating discussion of the relationship between biological, physical, and psychological rhythms ("Entrainment," pp. 161–175). An important, cross-cultural study of time and temporality. Appendixes, glossary of terms, bibliography.

110. **Halpern, Daniel, ed. On Nature: Nature, Landscape, and Natural History.**
San Francisco, CA: North Point Press, 1987.
319 pages.

Originally published in *Antaeus*, an international quarterly of literature (no. 57, 1986), this anthology features writings by some of the best nature writers in the field. Divided into five parts and consisting of twenty-three essays, the volume concludes with a separate booklist on available literature. Selections range from Annie Dillard's conversational "Total Eclipse" (pp. 160–169), to John Rodman's historical study "The Dolphin Papers" (pp. 252–282). Entries of particular interest to ecophilosophers are Edward O. Wilson's "Storm over the Amazon" (pp. 157–159); Noel Perrin's "Forever Virgin: The American View of America" (pp. 13–22), Leslie Silko's "Landscape, History, and the Pueblo Imagination" (pp. 236–243); and Joyce Oates' "Against Nature" (pp. 236–243).

111. **Hanson, Philip P., ed. Environmental Ethics: Philosophical and Policy Perspectives.**
Burnaby, B.C.: Simon Fraser University Press, 1986. 199 pages.

An anthology of seventeen papers relating moral considerations to environmental policies and concerns. An assortment of viewpoints are given— full contents of the work include: Charles Caccia, "Environmental Rights and Responsibilities"; Norman Morse, "An Environmental Ethic"; Stan Rowe, "In Praise of Beauty"; Philip Hanson, "Morality, Posterity, and Nature"; John Livingston, "Ethics as Prosthetics"; Stan Stein, "Ethics and the Justification of Environmental Policies"; Andrew Brook, "Ethics and Survival"; Tom Regan, "Honey Dribbles Down Your Fur"; Robert Van Hulst, "Against Sentimentalism"; Jan Narveson, "Against Animal Rights"; Wayne Sumner, "Sentience and Moral Standing"; Andrew Thompson and Anthony Dorcey, "Environmental Management as a Bargaining Process"; Fred Knelman, "Some Flaws and Biases in the Bargaining Process"; Gary Runka, "Bargaining as a Crucible for Environmental Ethics"; John O'Neill, "The Roots of Environmental Caring"; William Leiss, "Why We Do Not Need an Environmental Ethic"; David Copp, "Some Positions and Issues in Environmental Ethics." Notes, bibliography.

112. **Hardin, Garrett. Naked Emperors: Essays of a Taboo Stalker.** Los Alto, CA.: William Kaufman, 1982. 281 pages.

A collection of diverse writings on issues related to human ecology, immigration, and foreign aid. Hardin, a respected biologist, offers "heretical" or unorthodox judgments on these and other public issues, often recommending unpopular solutions to such problems as population control, emigration, environmental pollution, and sociobiology. Although Hardin's views are often inconsistent and at times even unconscionable, his work is nevertheless embraced by many ecophilosophers.

113. **Hardin, Garrett. Filter against Folly: How to Survive Despite Economists, Ecologists, and the Merely Eloquent.** New York, NY: Viking, 1985. 240 pages.

Hardin suggests that there are three really distinctive ways of examining the world: the "literate," the "numerate," and the "ecolate." He argues that unless economists, businessmen, and scientists begin to recognize all three views, the results will be ecologically disastrous. He extends his own "tragedy of the commons" discussion into this tripartite arena, illustrating the need for unifying different methods of resource management.

114. **Hargrove, Eugene C., ed. Religion and Environmental Crisis.** Athens, GA: University of Georgia Press, 1986. 248 pages.

To what extent does a particular religious orientation prevent (or contribute to) environmental degradation? Does the Judeo-Christian tradition, as currently practiced, promote or dissuade ecological stewardship? Can religion, in the modern world, advance a spirituality that is at once ecological and transcendent? These and other questions are the focus of this volume of ten essays by well-known theologians, environmental historians and philosophers. Essays by J. Donald Hughes, Susan Power Bratton, Po-keung Ip, Robert H. Ayers, Jonathan Helfand and John B. Cobb. Introduction by Frederick Ferré. Papers presented at a colloquium held at the University of Denver made possible by a grant from the Phillips Foundation of Minneapolis through the University of Denver's Center for Judaic Studies. A well edited anthology.

115. **Hargrove, Eugene C., ed. Beyond Spaceship Earth: Environmental Ethics and the Solar System.** San Francisco, CA: Sierra Club Books, 1987. 288 pages.

49

Fourteen essays by environmentalists and public figures read at a 1985 University of Georgia conference. A postpublication publicity blurb says that *Beyond Spaceship Earth* is "the first extensive exploration of the ethical and environmental issues involved in space exploration, [and] includes contributions from NASA and National Oceanic and Atmospheric Administration experts, and from other engineers, ecologists, philosophers, and medical and legal authorities." Attempts to answer such questions as "What are the commercial uses of space?" "Should strip mining be permitted on the moon?" and "Should we alter the atmosphere of Mars and Venus to make them hospitable to human life?" A necessarily speculative and tentative philosophical-ethical study of the solar system as the likely area of future environmental-ethical concerns. Illustrations.

116. **Hargrove, Eugene C. Foundations of Environmental Ethics.** Englewood Cliffs, NJ: Prentice-Hall, 1989 (in press).

A forthcoming volume, in three major parts, by the founder and editor of *Environmental Ethics*. The author looks at the ways in which the "history of ideas" has inadequately informed contemporary ecological thought and philosophy. After surveying the basic philosophical attitudes of the West, Hargrove begins building his environmental ethical foundations on the bedrock of aesthetic values found in nature, which, as he sees them, are axiologically antecedent to human values based in, say, economics or "unnatural" science. Contents of the work include: Part One, "Traditional Positions," which contains two chapters entitled "Philosophical Attitudes" and "Land-use Attitudes"; Part Two, "Environmental Positions," which discusses aesthetic, scientific, and wildlife protection attitudes, respectively; Part Three, "Philosophical Implications," which begins with a critique of traditional wildlife management practices and concludes with a chapter entitled "An Ontological Argument for Environmental Ethics"; and an Afterword, "Beyond Economics: Toward a Balanced Value System." An invaluable addition to the ecophilosophy library.

117. **Hart, John. The Spirit of the Earth: A Theology of the Land.** Ramsey, NJ: Paulist Press, 1984. 165 pages.

A Roman Catholic theologian argues for a more harmonious link between human needs and respect for the earth. The discussions cover four principal areas: land abuse, the ecological attitudes of the American Indians, Christian stewardship, the American political tradition. Hart's treatment of land use is a well-informed one, the author has served as Director of the Heartland Project—an agriculture mission endorsed by American Catholic Bishops. A common sense theological argument for Christian land use.

118. Hawley, Amos H. Human Ecology: A Theory of Community Structure. New York, NY: The Ronald Press, 1950. 456 pages.

The quintessential statement of human ecology, this volume develops a full and coherent theory of humanity's social embeddedness in the natural world. Hawley investigates the nature and development of community structure, the critical application of ecological principles to social phenomena. Because Hawley defines human ecology as a "fledgling discipline" (human ecology was 30 years old at the time), he admits that much of his work is programmatical. Chapter 15, an essay entitled "Temporal Aspects of Ecological Organization" (pp. 288–316), is unique in that it relates community structure to the temporal domains of natural cycles and physical durations. An anthropologically sound and well-documented book. Human Ecology. Anthropology.

119. Hearne, Vicki. Adam's Task: Calling Animals by Name. New York, NY: Alfred Knopf, 1986. 274 pages.

In this highly original work, the author, an assistant professor of English at Yale University, and a professional horse and dog trainer, argues for the "personhood" of domestic animals. She provides an informed defense of animals' capacity for understanding and commitment as well as a profound philosophical treatise on the nature of animal communication and behavior. Hearne's discussions take on standard academic theories about animals and animal thought while moving toward a more holistic interpretation of animal experience. A well-written, interdisciplinary narrative.

120. Heidegger, Martin. The Question Concerning Technology and Other Essays. Translated by William Lovitt. New York, NY: Harper & Row, 1977. 182 pages.

A student of Edmund Husserl, German philosopher Martin Heidegger is considered the central figure of modern existentialism. Though the focus of Heidegger's general philosophy is a phenomenological analysis of being, or *Dasein*, his work touches critically upon several areas of ecophilosophical inquiry—namely, dwelling and technology. In this assortment of essays, loosely collected around the theme of technology, Heidegger argues that there is an inherent danger of technology becoming a nature dominating force. "The essence of modern technology," writes Heidegger in the introductory essay, "lies in its (objectifying) enframing . . . " (p. 21). Considering the renewed interest in Heidegger's writings among ecophilosophers, this small volume should be a necessary addition to the environmental philosophy library.

121. **Henderson, Hazel. Politics of the Solar Age:**
The Alternatives to Economics. New York,
NY: Doubleday, 1981. 433 pages.

An insightful ecological critique of neoconservative, supply-side economics. Futurist Hazel Henderson borrows heavily from other thinkers: this volume is obviously indebted to the work of Barry Commoner, Sorokin, Georgescu-Roegen, E. F. Schumacher, and many others. While her study is copiously documented, Henderson's futurist philosophy is sometimes lacking for a more historically grounded base on which to stand. Without a past to referentially guide them, "alternative" economic practices are easily cooptable by the corporate elite and (as history has itself shown) lose their ability to effect recognizable change in the lived-world. Notes.

122. **Hendry, George S. Theology of Nature.**
Philadelphia, PA: Westminster Press, 1980.
258 pages.

A cosmological, political, and psychological examination of the theology of nature. Divided into three major parts, the book first explores the strengths and limitations of what he calls four nontheological approaches to nature. In part two, "Theology of Nature," Hendry repeatedly points to the ecological crisis as a reason for developing a rigorous nature theology. In part three, entitled "The Perception of Nature," the Christian view of the natural world is subsequently related to the four non-theological approaches presented in part one. A thorough statement of the biblical and historical Christian perception of nature.

123. **Highwater, Jamake. The Primal Mind: Vision**
and Reality in Indian America. New York,
NY: New American Library, 1981. 234 pages.

An eclectic book summarizing the author's personal views on two widely disparate cultures—the West's and his own Native American. Divided into three parts, the volume first introduces the nature and constitution of the primal mind. Part two, the largest portion of the work, looks at particular existential aspects of primal experience: imagery, time, place, motion, sound, identity. In chapter 3 of the second section, "Image" (pp. 55–88), Highwater asserts that the artist is the natural bridge between primitive intuitive orientations and the West's scientific rational ones. The remaining section,"The Future of the Primal Mind," consists of two short chapters offering possible scenarios for the preservation of indigenous peoples. Extensive bibliography.

124. **Horkheimer, Max, and Adorno, Theodor.**
Dialectic of Enlightenment. New York, NY:
Herder & Herder, 1972. 258 pages.

The classic critique of instrumental reason by the co-founders of the Institute for Social Research—The Frankfurt School. According to the authors' analysis, the rationality which grew out of the Enlightenment era became increasingly instrumental: it was concerned primarily with pragmatic technique and the technical colonization and control of humanity and nature. Reason, as such, no longer appealed to objective values, ideas, or greater moral goals but to the logic of manipulation and domination. This critique of instrumental reason has more recently been advanced by a number of ecophilosophers—Carolyn Merchant, Morris Berman, Fritjof Capra, Theodore Roszak, et al., have utilized, in one form or another, Horkheimer and Adorno's revolutionary critique of reason and science.

125. **Howard, Ted, and Rifkin, Jeremy. Who Should Play God?** New York, NY: Dell Publishing Co., 1977. 272 pages.

An alarming prophetic statement on the potential dangers of genetic engineering. According to the authors, because we are at the "crossroads of human history," biotechnology can no longer maintain its scientific and political secrecy. If we are to make informed rational judgments about the future of our species, we need to begin now the ethical debate surrounding the uses and abuses of biotechnological research. Since the publication of this book, genetic engineering has become *the raison d'être* of biological research. Unfortunately, many of the book's warnings have consequently either become realities or have been rendered obsolete by even newer biotechnological "advances." Notes. Bioethics.

126. **Hughes, J. Donald. Ecology in Ancient Civilizations.** Albuquerque, NM: University of New Mexico Press, 1975. 181 pages.

Many environmental historians have argued that a great deal of social and historical change is brought about by misuse of the environment. J. Donald Hughes shows that while the ancients were more directly dependent on the natural world than we are today, the consequences of their environmental misuse varied and often had many sides. While focusing mostly on the attitudes and practices of classical Greece and Rome, the author also describes the experiences of ancient Egyptians, Mesopotamians, Persians, Jews, and early Christians. Hughes examines the farming, hunting, grazing, mining, and treecutting practices of those ancient peoples, showing how their particular relationship to nature predetermined the scale and intensity of their sustenance technologies. Hughes gives additional information on the technology of the ancients and its broader ecological effects in chapter 12, "Ecology and the Fall of Rome" (pp. 128–140). For those who wish to know more about the ecology of the ancients, the suggestions for further reading provide a substantial bibliography. Maps, illustrations, color plates.

127. Hughes, J. Donald. American Indian Ecology.
El Paso, TX: Texas Western Press, 1983.
174 pages.

As the author points out in this important work, the American Indians had and have a unique understanding of place, an orderly and balanced perception of their living environment. Supporting his views with examples from many of the North American Indian tribes—especially those of the Southwest, the Northwest Coast, and the Great Plains, Hughes illustrates the sacred ecology of American Indian life. A sensitive and well-written document. Preface by Jamake Highwater. Illustrations, map.

128. Illich, Ivan. Toward a History of Needs. New
York, NY: Pantheon, 1977. 143 pages.

All five essays in this volume reflect Illich's thinking on the industrial mode of production and its profound effect on consciousness and culture. The essays are summarized in the introduction to this volume, most of which address issues raised in Illich's earlier work. For example, the first essay, "Useful Unemployment and Its Professional Enemies," is a postscript to problems raised in the author's earlier *Tools for Conviviality* (1973). In this essay, Illich discusses the myths surrounding industrial society and how those myths have become partly demystified by a new generation of concerned, well-informed individuals. The second essay is the text of a speech Illich delivered for the Canadian Foreign Policy Association in 1969, and addresses the major problems of Third World development. The remaining essays focus on the social and political consequences of modern production techniques and their specific effects on transportation, education, and health care. A good, albeit condensed, cross section of Illich's principal philosophy and concerns.

129. Illich, Ivan. Medical Nemesis. New York, NY:
Pantheon, 1976. 294 pages.

The fundamental thesis of this book, that modern medicine is itself a major threat to health, poses some basic questions about the direction of modern industrial society. The "medicalization of health," argues Illich, *creates* the conditions for disease, enhances and promotes unnecessary illness. As an example, it has been estimated that one out of every five patients admitted to a typical research hospital will acquire an illness generated by the medical care process itself. These iatrogenic illnesses, says Illich, have reached dangerous epidemic proportions: we must begin to seek out alternative health care techniques that allow for the natural healing processes of the body. Only with minimal technological intervention and maximum awareness of the environmental *gestalt* of virtuous health, can the nemesis of modern medicine be transcended. Concludes Illich: "Healthy people are those who live in healthy homes, on a healthy diet, in an environment equally fit for birth, growth, work, healing, and dying; they are sustained by a culture that enhances the conscious acceptance of limits to population, of aging, of incomplete recovery and ever-imminent death. Healthy people need minimum bureaucratic interference to mate, give birth, share the human condition and die" (pp. 274–75). Extensive notes.

130. **Illich, Ivan. Gender.** New York, NY: Pantheon, 1982. 192 pages.

As much a book on the vernacular domain of culture as a treatise on gender, Illich unravels the anthropological origins of the sexes; the ecological complementarity of their relationship in vernacular settings. In the book, Illich studies the history and evolution of gender through time, arguing that most contemporary theories of gender, including feminist ones, have produced equally sexist descriptions of the role of gender in construing reality. Modern theories of gender ignore the differentiating, dialectical distinction between male and female in all traditional cultures, and thus delineate the sexes into both "genderless" (read: productionist) and sexist frameworks. Because vernacular gender retains two distinct models from which men and women can conceptualize their universe, it fosters the most rudimentary conditions for social, psychological, and cultural expression. According to Illich, a coherent retention of those radically demarcated realities and domains, not an androgynous blending of them, constitutes the authentic vernacular milieu; the engendered reality of a preindustrial existence in harmony with nature. Extensive notes.

131. **Jackson, Barbara Ward, and Dubos, René. Only One Earth: The Care and Maintenance of a Small Planet.** New York, NY: Norton, 1972. 225 pages.

"An unofficial report commissioned by the Secretary General of the United Nations Conference on the Human Environment, prepared with the assistance of a 152-member committee of corresponding consultants in 58 countries" on global environmental policy and development. Notes and bibliography.

132. **Jackson, Wes. Altars of Unhewn Stone: Science and the Earth.** San Francisco, CA: North Point Press, 1987. 158 pages.

As an agriculture essayist, Jackson's work is exceptional: his prose equals that of Wendell Berry, whom he both admires and regularly collaborates with (Jackson and Berry are co-editors of *Meeting the Expectations of the Land*, 1984). In this volume of nineteen economically written essays, the author ponders the possibility of a science worthy of the earth and its natural biota. The musing leads towards the inception of a sustainable agriculture/land ethic that tries to mimic nature's rich diversity. Jackson is skeptical about the use of technology in agriculture, and in several of the essays criticizes recent developments in genetic engineering and molecular biology (See particularly "Land Wisdom vs. Lab Success," pp. 49–62). These new technological "advances" in the author's view, can only lead to the monoculturing of plant species, thereby reducing the level of biological organization to its lowest common denominator. The task of the future, environmentally conscious farmer, is to "simulate" the natural environment as closely as possible so that genetic variation is maximized to the greatest possible degree. Only then, proclaims Jackson, can we meet the true expectations of the land.

133. **Johnson, Warren. Muddling Toward Frugality.** Boulder, CO: Shambala, 1979. 252 pages.

Muddling Toward Frugality concerns the pace at which ecological lifestyles can be integrated into the "society-at-large." The term frugality in this book does not necessarily mean thriftiness, the abstention from luxury and lavishness. The author uses the term more in its original meaning—"to suggest economic conditions in which society is obliged by the force of circumstances to make full and 'fruitful' use of all its resources" (p. 12).

Johnson, a former professor of geography at San Diego University, insists that "muddling" (a slow and patient transition from affluent to frugal lifestyles) is necessary to maintain the integrity of the ecological approach (see chapter 5, "The Theory and Practice of Muddling," pp. 137–151). In chapter 7, "The Pace of Change" (pp. 171–202), Johnson provides the reader with what he sees as practical and workable time-frames for initiating ecologically sound economic and political policies. Johnson is aware of the possible hazards of "over-muddling," but he tends to underplay this issue.

His optimism for slow and methodical change too often downplays the urgency of more pressing ecological issues (acid rain, nuclear wastes, species extinction). Frugality in this work also seems to be viewed as a historical and economic imperative, something that is forced upon us by outside circumstances, scarce resources, a stingy nature. In any event, a persuasive argument for a steady and sustainable transformation from affluent to ecological sensibilities.

134. Jonas, Hans. The Phenomenon of Life:
Toward a Philosophical Biology. Chicago, IL:
University of Chicago Press, 1966 (Phoenix
edition, 1982). 303 pages.

Jonas' *The Phenomenon of Life* is an important book that is perhaps only now receiving the attention it deserves. It contains eleven essays on the "phenomenon of life," the relationship between the philosophy of organism and the philosophy of mind. "Put at its briefest," writes Jonas in his own introduction, "this volume offers an 'existential' interpretation of biological facts. Contemporary existentialism, obsessed with man alone, is in the habit of claiming as his unique privilege and predicament much of what is rooted in organic existence as such: in doing so, it withholds from the organic world the insights to be learned from the awareness of self. On its part, scientific biology, by its rules confined to the physical, outward facts, must ignore the dimensions of inwardness that belongs to life: in doing so, it submerges the distinction of 'animate' and 'inanimate.' A new reading of the biological record may recover the inner dimension—that which we know best—for the understanding of things organic and so reclaim for the psycho-physical unity of life that place in the theoretical scheme which it had lost through the divorce of the material and mental since Descartes" (p. ix). A well-articulated investigation of subjectivity that seeks to break through the anthropocentric confines of both idealist and existential philosophy as well as through the materialist confines of natural science.

135. Jonas, Hans. The Imperative of
Responsibility. In Search of an Ethics for the
Technological Age. Chicago, IL: University
of Chicago Press, 1984. 255 pages.

A critical search for an "ethics of responsibility" in the modern technological age. Jonas, the author of *The Phenomenon of Life* (1966), updates his earlier critiques of technology by applying his thoughts to recent technological advances. The responsibilities of humanity in their dealings with technology becomes ever greater, argues Jonas, because the new technologies (for example, biogenetic engineering) enables humans to manipulate the very substance of life; gives us the ultimate promethean power over nature. The first volume in a two-volume series. Philosophy of technology. Ethics.

136. Joranson, Philip N., and Butigan, Ken eds.
Cry of the Environment: Rebuilding the
Christian Creation Tradition. Santa Fe, NM:
Bear & Company, 1984. 476 pages.

An essential volume for anyone interested in the historical relationship between the Judeo-Christian tradition and our present environmental crisis.

In twenty-five scholarly chapters, the book calls for a revisioning of "creation consciousness" so that Christian worship includes all living entities and life-forms—including humans. While many of the contributors acknowledge that the Christian view of nature has not always been an environmentally conscious one, there is agreement that environmental awareness in Christian thought is, historically speaking, prevalent enough to dispel the common belief that Christianity has been responsible for environmental degradation.

An enormous amount of evidence is compiled to support a creation-centered ethic in Christian doctrine; Richard Woods, for example, cites the traditions of the patristic fathers and Celtic monastic orders in illustrating the influential role of nature in the early Christian church (pp. 62–84). Paul Weigand reinterprets the life and work of Saint Francis—the patron Saint of ecology—as the most *radically* respectful toward others and the created world (pp. 148–157).

A more modern defense is John B. Cobb's, who offers here an abbreviated version of his well-known "process theology." Citing Alfred North Whitehead's "philosophy of organism" as the most ecologically sound basis for recovering the unity of God's creation with the human world, Cobb invites Christians to take responsibility for the lives of other creatures. The ecotheology that results is one that allows for the development of a relational awareness between (1) naturalistic occurrences and divine events, (2) ecological wisdom and spiritual compassion. Other notable contributions by Bernard Anderson, Matthew Fox, Paul Lutz, Conrad Bonifazi, Douglas Adams, and Philip Joranson. Project sponsored by the Center for Ethics and Social Policy, Berkeley, California. Foreword by Ian G. Barbour.

137. **Juenger, Georg Friedrich. The Failure of Technology.** Chicago, IL: Regnery Gateway, 1949. 189 pages.

In the modern age, technology has the ability to order, control, and even destroy the lifeworld of the planet. The splitting of the atom and the splicing of the gene has enabled humankind to dominate nature in ways never before possible. Yet as self-evident as the destructive power of technology appears to our present age, there are only a handful of sustained studies on the deleterious effects of technology on the human order. One of these studies is Juenger's seminal *The Failure of Technology*, which has influenced such thinkers as Martin Heidegger and Jacques Ellul.

Few writers have warned against the destructive power of technology as consistently and thoughtfully as Friedrich Juenger has in this small volume. In the work, the author asserts that technology, in its claims to totalizing efficiency, "purges nature of life and man of humanity" (p. xi.). He sees technology as reducing life—via technique and technical rationality—to mathematical abstractions and casual mechanisms. Admittedly, Juenger concentrates exclusively on the demonic and destructive power of technology; nevertheless, one should view the work as an essential critique of the technological worldview. Introduction by Frederick Wilhelmson.

138. **Kaufman, Les, and Mallory, Kenneth, eds. The Last Extinction.** Cambridge, MA: The MIT Press, 1986. 208 pages.

A six-chapter study of the relationship between species extinction and human activity. Explores such topics as the loss of species diversity, the problems inherent in trying to preserve endangered species in artificial environments, and the devastation in tropical rainforests. Concludes with an essay by David Ehrenfeld which suggests a possible transformation in the way we perceive our relationship to nature. A valuable contribution to the growing literature on extinction. Suggested reading lists, illustrations, list of organizations involved in species preservation.

139. **Keller, Evelyn Fox. Reflections on Gender and Science.** New Haven, CT: Yale University Press, 1985. 193 pages.

The role of gender in the construction of science and views of nature has been a major interest of recent scholarship. In this book, Keller examines the "genderization of science," attempting to construct a scientific worldview void of gender stereotypes and androcentric images of nature. Each of the nine essays that make up the book deal with the masculinization of our categories of experience—in the first section Keller discusses these categories from a historical perspective; in the second, psychoanalytically; in the third, from within science itself. Keller concludes that we must transcend the gender stereotypes of modern science and rely on a mode of inquiry grounded in a respect and empathy with nature. An empathetic science, concludes the author, would not dominate nature as an "objective other," but would resurrect nature as a knowable, yet unobjectifiable, partner.

140. **Kelly, Petra. Fighting for Hope.** Translation by Marianne Howarth. West Germany: South End Press, 1984. 121 pages.

A founding member of West Germany's Green Party (Die Grünen) discusses its political present and future. Kelley documents the ecological and peace movements rise to influence in the German *Bundestag*, focusing heavily on the role of women in establishing the party (See particularly "Women and Ecology," pp. 101–108). Introduction by Heinrich Boll.

141. **Kimes, Maymie B., and William F., eds. The Complete John Muir: A Reading**

Bibliography. Fresno, CA: Panorama West, 1986. 208 pages.

An ambitious attempt to gather all substantial references to Muir's work, including books, periodicals, letters, and interviews. Containing well over six hundred entries, each entry includes standard bibliographic information along with a physical description of each work. The product of over thirty years of research by the authors. Arranged chronologically, cross-referenced.

142. **Kohák, Erazim. The Embers and the Stars: A Philosophical Inquiry into the Moral Sense of Nature.** Chicago, IL: The University of Chicago Press, 1984. 269 pages.

An ambitious and inspiring work. A Husserlian scholar and professor of philosophy at Boston University, Kohák poetically discloses the moral dimensions of the natural milieu. In the history of Western philosophy, nature has taken many shapes and forms, the author's ability to capture and articulate the variety of human/nature experiences is extraordinary. Kohák's ecophenomenology does not ignore the many transcendental pitfalls of classical phenomenological literature, either. He generally overcomes the apolitical quietism of the genre by laying out a rigorous personalistic ontology, critically addressing the possible aporias of an ecological "right praxis."

The text is divided into five philosophically arranged divisions: "Theoria," "Physis," "Humanitas," "Skepsis," and "Credo." A sampling of chapter titles include: "The Gift of the Moral Law" (Part 2), "A Philosophy of Personalism" (Part 3), "The Vertigo of History" (Part 4), and "Being, Time, and Eternity" (Part 5). Despite the fact that *The Embers and the Stars* is "a philosopher's book, deeply indebted to the cultural heritage of three millennia of Western thought," the book's prose is neither pedantic nor entirely inaccessible to the layman (p. xi). A landmark book for ecophilosophy. Contains an annotated index of topics, extensive notes.

143. **LaChapelle, Dolores. Earth Wisdom.** Silverton, CO: Way of the Mountain Center, 1978. 183 pages.

A philosophical guidebook for ecological "reinhabitation," *Earth Wisdom* deals with the need to heal the split between human consciousness and nature. LaChapelle touches upon a variety of collateral subjects: the art of skiing powder snow, Tai Chi, Martin Heidegger, and American Indian rituals. The author's primary message is that ritual is essential for sustainable ecological practice—ritual intimately connects the human organism to his fellow beings and to the larger natural environment. Ecological ritual—earth wisdom—concludes LaChapelle, provides the necessary religious tool for locating ourselves within the natural world; helps us to think logically, analogically, and ecologically about our existential relationship to the earth. Illustrations.

144. **Large, Martin, H.C. Social Ecology: Exploring Postindustrial Society.** Gloucester, England: M. H. Large, 1981. 162 pages.

A follower of the organic philosophy of Rudolph Steiner looks at the relationship between community, consciousness, and social organization in post-industrial society. Notes, bibliography.

145. **Lee, Dorothy. Freedom and Culture.** Englewood, Cliffs, NJ: Prentice Hall, 1959. 179 pages.

A classic anthropological statement on the existential realities of primitive culture—the author compares and contrasts the individual and social realities of modern and primitive life. Throughout the work Lee maintains that individual freedom and personal autonomy can be won only in the participated security of organic, tightly-knit social groups. Select chapters include: "Individual Autonomy and Social Structure" (pp. 5–14), "Personal Significance and Group Structure" (pp. 15–26), "Responsibility Among the Dakotas" (pp. 5969), "Being and Value in Primitive Culture" (pp. 89–104), "The Conception of Self Among Wintu Indians" (pp. 131–141), "View of the Self in Greek Culture" (pp. 141–153). Notes.

146. **Leiss, William. The Domination of Nature.** New York, NY: George Braziller, 1972. 242 pages.

William Leiss, a philosopher and student of Herbert Marcuse, provides a penetrating analysis of historical and theoretical attitudes toward nature. The book is distinguished by its historical treatment and critical conclusions regarding technology: we should not regard the essence of human technique simply as our ability to dominate nature; rather, we should view technique as the mastery of the relationship between nature and humanity. Although Leiss' proposals to meet our contemporary environmental crisis are often ambiguous and abstract, this book is recommended for its critical explication of the human/nature relationship. Notes.

147. **Leopold, Aldo. Sand County Almanac: And Sketches Here and There.** New York, NY: Oxford University Press, 1987 (Special Commemorative Edition). 228 pages.

Originally published in 1949, this classic work has influenced four decades of environmental thought. Leopold's infamous "land-ethic" is found here (chapter 6, pp. 201–226) as is a number of incisive statements about humanity's duty to preserve the natural world. The dialogue follows the comings and goings of a year in the Wisconsin countryside, accentuated with philosophical musings and intellectual asides. Leopold sums up the work nicely in his own introduction to the book, stating that "[t]here are some who can live without wild things, and some who cannot. These essays are the delights and dilemmas of one who cannot" (p. vii). Introduction by Robert Finch.

148. **LeShan, Lawrence, and Margenau, Henry.**
Einstein's Space & Van Gogh's Sky. New
York, NY: McMillan Publishing Co., 1983.
268 pages.

Lawrence LeShan, a research psychologist, and Henry Margenau, professor of physics and philosophy at Yale University, explore the new scientific discoveries that supposedly reveal the fundamental links between physical reality and human consciousness. Divided into three parts: (1) "The Meaning of Reality," (2) "The Search for Scientific Truth," (3) "Domains of the Social Sciences," this volume demonstrates the limitations of the conventional view of reality and offers alternative visions for further inquiries about the nature of Nature.

In the book's second chapter, "Structures of Reality," the authors claim that the Renaissance worldview, as defined by Descartes, organized and separated "objective and subjective perceptions and divided the objective [realm] into such specialties as physics, chemistry, biology, and sociology" (p. 30). According to the authors, this separation of reality into objective and subjective spheres, "led to tremendous advances in knowledge, prediction, and control of the 'objective' world. . . . The division of reality into a sphere of matter—the *res extensa*—and a sphere of mind—the *res cogitans*—provided a very powerful methodology of the study of one and a very inadequate methodology for the study of the other. As we can see now but could not have predicted then, the imbalance had inexorable and unfortunate consequences. Our power to manipulate and control the 'outside' world—matter and energy—advanced greatly, but we made no advances in the understanding of our own behavior and our inner experience" (pp. 30–31). This imbalance in the organization of experience, concludes the authors, created a vast increase in our knowledge of medicine and physics, which also made the population of our species increase at an astounding rate—"greatly developed our power to destroy ourselves and the balance with nature" (p. 32). Other notable chapters are 3, "Varieties of Human Experience," and 16, "The Domain of Ethics." Notes.

149. **Levin, David Michael. The Body's Recollection of Being: Phenomenological Psychology and the Deconstruction of Nihilism. Boston, MA: Routledge & Kegan Paul, 1985. 390 pages.**

A unique study of the phenomenology of the body, its chthonic grounding in the earth, its creative dance with nature's rhythms and periodicities. In his interpretation of experience as corporeal embodiment, Levin draws heavily from the work of Merleau-Ponty, Heidegger, Nietzche, Jung, Dewey, and Freud. Chapters 6 and 7 should be of noted interest to ecophilosophers as Levin reflects on the "ground of being"—the relationship of the body to the earth, soil, and lived space.

In chapter 7, "The Gathering Round Dance" (pp. 317–349), Levin explores our present relationship to space and place, arguing that we have devalued or eliminated all bodily felt awareness of our spatial environments. "[W]e have spatialized the world of our dwelling in a space that is indifferent to our deepest needs and concerns," writes the author. "Our entanglement with the objective space of classical physics has in fact *encouraged* us to deny, to forget, or to devalue our pre-ontological, bodily felt sense of the intrinsic richness, meaningfulness, and openness of our space for living. Who can dispute the fact that the sway of this conception has made it considerably more difficult for us to experience the receptivity of our space to the healthy emotional needs, feelings and concerns that would most fulfill us as human beings? We have expanded our civilization into the envelope of outer space; yet we cannot make room, here on earth, for people very different from ourselves. We control a far reach of space; yet we still have no resting place, no near abode, for the weary and desperate soul. We 'contact' the most distant stars, but do so in a space without any room for deeply meaningful feeling, since the spatial uniformity which makes such contact possible derives from a theoretical framework that *requires* the relinquishing of qualitative, bodily felt experience" (p. 346). Extensive notes and bibliography.

150. **Levins, Richard, and Lewontin, Richard. The Dialectical Biologist. Cambridge, MA: Harvard University Press, 1985. 303 pages.**

According to the authors (two Harvard biologists), the purpose of presenting this collection of essays was to challenge the assumptions of Cartesian reductionism in biological and evolutionary theory. Biological systems, argue the authors, do not exist simply as an interpenetration of parts and wholes, subjects and objects. This conception renders the biological "subject" passive without a sufficient role in the evolutionary process. The actual role of the organism is quite different: it both makes and is made by its environment and is thus an active participant in its own evolutionary history. Organisms are both the subjects and objects of evolution. Includes additional chapters on the social and political dimensions of science, and ends with a general discussion of dialectical theory's history and philosophical pedigree.

151. **Levy-Leboyer, Claude. Psychology and Environment.** Translation by David Canter and Ian Griffiths. London, England: Sage Publications, 1982. 197 pages.

A psychological investigation of the human-natural environment. The author, an environmental psychologist, is currently vice president of the Université René Descartes in Paris, France. Although she borrows from a number of ecological methodologies, her approach utilizes primarily perceptual models. Environmental psychology, bibliography.

152. **Linberg, David C., and Numbers, Ronald L., eds. God and Nature: Historical Essays on the Encounter between Christianity and Science.** Berkeley, CA: University of California Press, 1986. 516 pages.

An outgrowth of an international conference on the historical relations of Christianity and science, this anthology makes an important contribution to our understanding of the historical relationship between faith, science, nature, and reason. These issues are important for ecophilosophy because of the identification of science with Christian attitudes toward nature—attitudes that are said to influence even our modern conceptions about the natural world. If God is immanent in nature, as a number of Christian theologians have argued, then one must treat creation with a certain amount of respect and dignity. If God created the world *ex nihilo* and remains separate from it, then the study of nature—through science and reason—can be morally justified. In either case, scientific inquiry is dependent on the recognition of a "divine order" in nature and thus the relationship between science and religion is much more of an interdependent than separate one. The eighteen chapters that comprise the work look closely at this relationship, analyzing the various ways in which religious thought and scientific activity are historically and dialectically akin. Notes.

153. **Linzey, Andrew. Christianity and the Rights of Animals.** New York, NY: Crossroads Publishing, 1987. 197 pages.

Linzey, the Director of Studies at the Center for the Study of Theology at the University of Essex, is also the author of one of the earliest Christian studies on animal rights and welfare (*Animal Rights: A Christian Assessment*, 1976). In this more recent work, the author develops the idea of a rights theory aligned more to creation-centered doctrine.

This new approach, which involves what Linzey has coined "theos-rights," calls for the protection of animals out of responsibility to God's creation. Under this conception animals have rights only in the sense that are part of God's greater covenant. For Linzey, to affirm animals as possessors of rights means that: (1) God as creator has rights in his creation; (2) that Spirit-filled, breathing creatures, composed of flesh and blood, are subjects of inherent value to God; and (3) that these animals can make an objective moral claim which is nothing less than God's claim upon us (p. 69).

Concerning levels of sentience, Linzey gives greater value to creatures that most resemble humans, which leads the author into a kind of "mammalocentricity." While not denying that lower life forms have sentience, he at the same time cannot extend these creatures "theos-rights" because they are not "known to possess spiritually analogous lives to those of humans" (p.84). Appendix: "Church Statements on Animals." Guide to further reading. Extensive notes.

154. **Livingston, John A. The Fallacy of Wildlife Conservation.** Toronto: McClelland and Stewart, 1981. 126 pages.

Livingston, a Canadian poet and naturalist, takes a hard look at conventional approaches to wildlife conservation. He finds most of them to be tragically destructive, as much a threat to nature as a means to stop the exploitation of it. He says that most conservation techniques, under the rubric of bureaucratic environmentalism, co-opt the principles of ecology for the continuation of corporate development. The tenets of modern conservation strategies only minimize or slow down the destruction of wildlife, they do very little to actually stop environmental degradation. Throughout the text, Livingston criticizes the arguments for "minimal impact," the conventional view of wildlife "management," the anthropocentric biases of contemporary conservation practices. Written in a nonpedantic heuristic style, the book is full of provocative ideals and should be of important interest to all environmental philosophers.

155. **Lovelock, J.E. Gaia: A New Look at Life on Earth.** New York, NY: Oxford University Press, 1979. 157 pages.

The Gaia hypothesis (from the Greek Earth goddess *Ge*) suggests that the conditions for life on earth display the behavior of a simple organism, perhaps a living creature—Gaia. In this provocative small book, Lovelock, a British organic chemist, attempts to demonstrate how Gaia has been formed by a self-regulating entity, with the capacity to control and maintain the optimal living conditions for life on this planet. Occasionally, Lovelock's personal and engaging discussion borders on the mythological; more frequently, the unapologetically cybernetic. Overall, the text reads much better as a simple ethical statement about caring for the fragile earth than as a rigorous scientific theory of modern biology. Glossary.

156. **MacCormack, C., and Strathem, M., eds. Nature, Culture, and Gender.** Cambridge, MA: Cambridge University Press, 1980. 227 pages.

The relationship between nature and culture has become increasingly scrutinized by contemporary ecofeminist theoreticians. The commonly held assumption that nature is to culture as female is to male, does not seem to be universally valid according to recent anthropological research. *Nature, Culture, and Gender* represents initial research into this area of inquiry; the eight essays in this collection attempt to build a stronger foundation upon which to erect theories about the relationship of gender to nature and culture. The essay by Jordanova, "Natural Facts: A Historical Perspective on Science and Sexuality" (chapter 3), does a thorough job of defining some of the more historical and environmental problems involved in separating gender from culture and science. Jordanova's essays, and most of the other seven, however, are framed in a largely anthropological idiom. Nevertheless, the ecophilosopher should find these studies on the male-female, human-nature relationships essential additions to the ecophilosophical literature. Notes.

157. **Magel, Charles R. A Bibliography of Animal Rights and Related Matters.** Lanham, MD: University Press of America, 1981. 622 pages.

A comprehensive and invaluable work, listing 3,210 entries related to animal rights and animal rights theory. The literature on animals is arranged temporally, beginning with materials from Aristotle, Lucretius, Plato, The Old Testament, and Pythagoras. The bulk of the entries, however, are from twentieth century sources. Magel also lists the specialized publications of virtually all organizations concerned with animals, the organizations themselves, cookbooks (vegetarian, of course), and magazines and journals. Because the majority of the entries are *not* annotated, this massive text is, at times, overwhelming to the reader. Beyond this minor complaint, the bibliography has few flaws and should be of immeasurable usefulness to future research in this field. Index.

158. **Mannison, Don; McRobbie, Michael; and Routley, Richard, eds. Environmental Philosophy.** Canberra: Australian National

University, Research School of Social Sciences, Department of Philosophy, 1980. 385 pages.

An excellent anthology of essays resulting from two Australian conferences on environmental ethics in 1977 and 1978. The majority of the text contains the exhaustive arguments of Richard and Val Routley on human chauvinism and "class" anthropocentricism. Human chauvinism, argues the married couple, prefers humans over all other natural classes; without sufficient reason. The Routley's further argue that we need to radically extend moral concern to nonhumans—plants, animals, ecosystems. However, some ecophilosophers, have criticized them for suggesting "the removal of humans from a dominant position in the natural order" (p. 189). Other notable contributions by Robert Elliot and William Godfrey-Smith, Roger Lamb, Lloyd Reinhardt, and H.J. McCloskey. An important book for those doing serious ecophilosophical research.

159. **Marcuse, Herbert. One-Dimensional Man.**
Boston. MA: Beacon Press, 1964. 260 pages.

Herbert Marcuse studied philosophy at the Universities of Berlin and Freiburg, at the latter with Edmund Husserl and Martin Heidegger. In the early 1930's he began his work with Max Horkheimer as a founding member of the Institute for Social Research–The Frankfurt School. In *One-Dimensional Man*, one of Marcuse's last major works, the author extends the critical theory of the Frankfurt School into his own critique of the power of technological rationality and domination.

The underlying conception of Marcuse's study is that the domination of nature through science and technology gives rise to a new form of human domination. "Society reproduced itself in a growing technical ensemble of things and relations which included the technological utilization of men—in other words, the struggle for existence and the exploitation of man and nature became ever more scientific and rational" (p. 146). This increasingly scientific-technological rationality quantifies nature, separates reality "from all inherent ends . . . the true from the good, science from ethics" (p. 40).

At times, Marcuse's analysis seems a bit too general and all-inclusive—it tends to be deterministic insofar as it presumes the level at which technology represses all and every aspect of life. The technological rationality of *One-Dimensional Man* condemns all science to domination, all domination to the domination of nature via the technological *a priori* of objective reason. Technique is not always an all-pervasive system, self-contained and deterministic, but is also immersed in a social world of intentions and interactions; and is often a necessary condition for liberatory practice and personal freedom. The problem of one-dimensionality may not be a question of whether technique and domination are co-dependent as simply one of human domination.

160. **Marsh, George Perkins. The Earth as Modified by Human Action.** New York, NY: Arno Press, 1970. (Originally published in 1874). 656 pages.

Long before the word ecology became fashionable, George Perkins Marsh was writing about the ecological relationship between humankind and nature. In 1864 he presented an earlier version of this work, *Man and Nature*, which he later revised and lengthened into *The Earth as Modified by Human Action*. Although Marsh is regarded by many to be the patron saint of the environmental movement, his initial motivation for wilderness preservation was primarily utilitarian. For example, Marsh was not opposed to the artificial modification of nature—he believed that God made the world for the use of man; that the human race is not only above, but apart from, the rest of creation. Despite Marsh's utilitarian stewardship position, one must still recognize that *Man and Nature* is, in the words of Lewis Mumford, "the fountainhead of the conservation movement."

161. **Marx, Leo. The Machine in the Garden: Technology and the Pastoral Idea in America.** New York, NY: Oxford University Press, 1964. 392 pages.

Few have analyzed the historical and contemporary dichotomy between technology and the pastoral ideal in America as has Leo Marx in his well known study. The author approaches his subject matter from the point of view of the literary and social historian, discussing the writings of Virgil, Shakespeare, Thoreau, Hawthorne, Melville, Mark Twain, Henry James, Henry Adams, and others. Like Roderick Nash and John Seelye, Marx recognizes the complementary relation of pastoralism with the American ideal of "New Jerusalem." The Puritan millennial vision, observes Marx, at once implied the use of transformational technique and utopian communalism. An excellent historical summary of the dialectic between technology and the pastoral idea in American thought. Extensive notes, illustrations.

162. **McCloskey, H. J. Ecological Ethics and Politics.** Totawa, NJ: Rowman and Littlefield, 1983. 167 pages.

Henry McCloskey, of La Trobe University, Australia, is the author of a number of books and articles on normative and meta-ethics. In this work, McCloskey rejects environmentalists' claims that a radically new ecological ethic is necessary, and argues that we should pursue an ecological ethics based only on our obligations to human rights and welfare. He does, however, address the issue of whether and how environmental problems can be effectively resolved without sacrificing human freedoms and liberal democracy. The author's skepticism, his darkly colored view of the liberating potentials of a rigorous ecological ethic/praxis, does affect his normative and political claims from the onset, however. In spite of some gross misconceptions about the ecological *Weltanschauung*, the book is valuable—a healthy balance to some of the less human-centered tracts in the ecophilosophical corpus.

163. **McLean, George F. Man and Nature.**
New York, NY: Oxford University Press, 1979.
240 pages.

Consisting of papers read in 1976 at the second conference of the International Society for Metaphysics in West Bengal, India, *Man and Nature* seeks "the development of metaphysical insight which will enable man to direct progress, face the limitations of the physical world and achieve a more adequate fulfillment of himself (*sic*) in nature" (p. xv). The eighteen papers of this volume are divided into four parts: (1) "Science and Nature," (2) "Progress and Nature," (3) "Person and Nature," and (4) "Transcendence and Nature." Selected papers include John E. Smith's "Nature as Object and as Environment: The Pragmatic Outlook" (pp. 50–57); S. C. Thakur's "A Touch of Animism" (pp. 131-142); Chang Chung-Yuan's "The Nature of Man as Tao" (pp. 143–153); and Bishnupada Bhattacharya's "Aesthetic Meaning of Nature: An Indian Approach" (pp. 215–231). Because the papers represent a wide variety of philosophical traditions from both Eastern and Western thought, the depth at which important axiological issues can be discussed remains limited. In any event, *Man and Nature* provides a valuable contribution to the study of *Homo sapiens*, nature, and metaphysics.

164. **McPhee, John. Encounters with the Archdruid.** New York, NY: Farrar, Straus and Giroux, 1971. 245 pages.

The majority of this well-known author's work is a unique blend of natural history and human opinion. McPhee's writing concerns both human and natural landscapes as well as the sometimes antagonistic relationship between the two. A prolific writer, the author has produced more than a dozen books on human and natural themes, including *Rising from the Plains* (1986), *Table of Contents* (1985), and *The Pine Barrens* (1968). The work in question is perhaps the reviewer's favorite, which deals with David Brower, the former director of the Sierra Club, and his close encounters with individuals not equally committed to "saving the earth." The book's narratives take place in three different wilderness areas—the sea islands of south Georgia, the Glacier Peak Wilderness in the Cascades, and on the Colorado River—and address many of the same questions confronting conservation philosophy today: Should humans develop wilderness? And if so, to what degree?

165. **Meeker, Joseph. The Comedy of Survival: Studies in Literary Ecology.** New York, NY: Scribner's and Sons, 1974. 217 pages.

An intellectual application of biological and ecological principles to literary studies. The author asserts that the tragedy genre has perennially treated man as separate from nature—projects a model of human doom and ecological catastrophe. Meeker contrasts the "tragic hero" concept of classical literature with the "comic hero" model, concluding that it is the comic hero, the buffoon, who is more friendly toward life and who seeks an equilibrium of man and nature; the adjustment to, rather than the transformation of, the natural world. Illustrations.

166. **Merchant, Carolyn. The Death of Nature: Women, Ecology, and the Scientific Revolution.** San Francisco, CA: Harper & Row, 1980. 348 pages.

A historian of science critically reassesses the scientific revolution of the sixteenth and seventeenth centuries in this well-known volume. Merchant explores the historical and cultural connections between women's issues and ecology, science and environmental degradation. According to the author, nature was still seen as a living organism prior to the scientific revolution. But when the scientific revolution gradually replaced the organic vision of nature with a mechanistic one, the earth could no longer be perceived as a living entity, a nurturing mother to be cherished and protected. Under the rubric of mechanistic science, nature soon became a disembodied entity, a separate reality that could be manipulated and destroyed through scientific and technological means. The death and disenchantment of nature through the widespread acceptance of the mechanical order eventually meant that knowing and being were also separate from nature.

In chapter 9, "Mechanism as Power" (pp. 216–235), Merchant lists five philosophical assumptions of the mechanistic worldview; the models of being, knowledge, and method that make possible the human manipulation and control of nature. They are as follows: (1) Matter is composed of particles (the ontological assumption), (2) The universe is a natural order (the principle of identity), (3) Knowledge and information can be abstracted from the natural world (the assumption of context independence), (4) Problems can be analyzed into parts that can be manipulated by mathematics (the methodological assumption), (5) Sense data are discrete (the epistemological assumption) (p. 228). An important document for ecophilosophy. Illustrations (24 plates). Extensive notes.

167. **Metcalf, William James. The Environmental
Crisis: A Systems Approach.** New York, NY:
St. Martin's Press, 1977. 150 pages.

Based on the author's M.A. thesis which was completed in 1975 at the
University of Queensland, *The Environmental Crisis* attempts an integrated
and interdisciplinary approach to solving the world's ecological problems.
Metcalf's heuristic, perhaps reductionistic, method is grounded in "systems
theory," or more specifically, "on what is known of the workings of natural
systems" (p. 31). This approach, based on four primary elements or "subsys-
tems" (ethics, environment, lifestyle, and technology), attempts to combine
these factors into a comprehensive understanding of environmental
problems—as well as their potential solutions. Metcalf's is primarily an introductory statement, the ethical "subsystem," for example, is given only
minor treatment (chapter 8, pp. 69–86). Notes and comprehensive bibliography.

168. **Midgley, Mary. Beast and Man: The Roots
of Human Nature.** Ithaca, NY: Cornell
University Press, 1978. 377 pages.

Unburdened by the technical jargon pervading most analytical accounts
of human and animal behavior, *Beast and Man* argues quite convincingly
that we must understand ourselves as continuous, rather than separate from,
the rest of the animal kingdom. In fact, ecophilosopher Midgley believes that
in order to fully understand human nature, comparisons between human
beings and other animal species are crucial. The book is arranged accordingly in five parts, consisting of (1) a conceptual analysis of human nature, (2)
a lengthy examination of how we should study this nature, (3) the practical
and ethical consequences of having this particular nature, (4) the traditional
characteristics separating humans from other animals, and (5) the ethical and
moral importance of understanding ourselves as part of the biosphere. Offers
some insightful and artful arguments against some of the philosophical writings of E. O. Wilson, Desmond Morris, Descartes, John Paul Sartre, Spinoza,
and others. Comprehensive notes.

169. **Midgley, Mary. Animals and Why They
Matter: A Journey Around the Species
Barrier.** Athens, GA: University of Georgia
Press, 1984. 158 pages.

A philosophical exploration, in mostly a nontechnical manner, on the way
we think about the differences between ourselves and other animals. Contains discussions of Kant and the Rationalist tradition, David Hume, John
Stuart Mill, Rousseau, Jane Goodall, Gilbert Ryle, and many others. An in-

troductory essay, "Getting Animals in Focus" (pp. 9–18), begins by asking the reader to take seriously our moral and ethical relations with other animals.

After deftly discussing such issues as competition, sentimentality, and the Rationalist tradition, chapter 7, entitled "Women, Animals, and Other Awkward Cases" (pp. 74–88), provides a unique historical perspective on the symbolic relationship between sexism and speciesism. Midgley concludes this elegantly written, uncompromisingly rigorous synthesis of political philosophy, comparative psychology, and analytic philosophy, with substantial essays on anthropocentrism and the subjectivity and consciousness of animals. Perhaps the only flaw in this otherwise flawless book is Midgley's failure to adequately defend her position on giving considerable interests to animals as opposed to humans—the proper amount or why. Notes.

170. **Miller, Harlan B., and Williams, William H.**
Ethics and Animals. Clifton, NJ: Human
Press, 1983. 416 pages.

A comprehensive anthology presenting a wide and impressive range of views on the treatment of nonhuman animals. Originally presented at the conference, The Moral Foundations of Public Policy: Ethics and Animals, held at Virginia Polytechnic Institute in 1979, the papers discuss everything from the theoretical and normative explorations of the moral status of animals to the ethics of eating meat, vivisection, and zoos. (Generally, a variety of viewpoints is presented on each subject.) There are contributions by the usual animal liberation vanguard, e.g. Tom Regan, Bernard Rollin, and Stephen Clark, as well as contributions by lesser-known advocates of nonhuman rights (Jan Narueson, Annette Baier, Peter Wenz). This collection is also unique in that it includes several arguments advancing the ultimate supremacy of human interests over animal interests. Excellent bibliography.

171. **Mitcham, Carl, and Grote, Jim. Theology and**
Technology: Essays in Christian Analysis
and Exegesis. Lanham, MD: University Press
of America, 1984. 521 pages.

A three-part analysis of the relationship of technology to theological, epistemological, and philosophical considerations. Following lengthy introductory essays by the two editors, Part I outlines the basic issues surrounding the question of technology as related to questions of faith and reason in Christian exegesis. These five essays look closely at the Christian tradition as benefactor to, or opponent of, technique and technical rationality. Many of the authors conclude that a strong case can be made for associating the most vital periods of Christian life and work with anti-technological attitudes, especially those attitudes advanced by the Anabaptists and Puritans.

Part II, which represents the bulk of the text (twelve essays) explores further the relationship between theological positions and technological achievements. Several of the contributors to this section relate technology as directly antithetical to Christian belief and practice; P. Hans Sun, for example, sees technology—in opposition to prayer—as a system actively bent on controlling the external environment (pp. 171–192). Part III, a "Select Bibliography of Theology and Technology," is an annotated listing of over five hundred readings related to both theological and technological themes, including a section devoted entirely to "Religious Environmental Ethics" (pp. 441–470). A well-presented and carefully edited volume. Notes, epilogue.

172. **Muir, John. Wilderness Essays.** Salt Lake City,
UT: Peregrine Smith Books, 1980. 288 pages.

The Peregrine Smith publishing house has brought forth a number of volumes that should be of particular interest to ecophilosophers. This reprint of John Muir's *Wilderness Essays* is certainly one of them. Provides ten of Muir's most important essays, including "The Discovery of Glacier Bay," "Near View of the High Sierra," and "The Animals of Yosemite."

173. **Mumford, Lewis. The Myth of the Machine: Technics and Human Development.** New
York, NY: Harcourt Brace Jovanovich, 1966.
342 pages.

One of Lewis Mumford's best-known studies on the historical and cultural origins of technological and human development. Mumford provides a comprehensive, almost encyclopedic view of the relationship between man and machine from paleolithic to modern times. Instead of simply tracing the origins of human culture in terms of our command of tools and conquest of nature, Mumford demonstrates how tools usually evolve *a posteriori* out of changes in human ritual, language, and social organization. The author's treatment of the material follows a historical sequence, but each chapter, from the prologue to the last, embraces the past, present, and future development of human technics. In many respects, Mumford's work predates the attempts of ecophilosophy to re-emerge the human into the natural world—*The Myth of the Machine* is a major statement on the social, cultural, and historical foundations of technology and human technique. Extensive annotated bibliography.

174. **Naess, Arne. Ecology, Community, and Life Style.** Cambridge, MA: Cambridge
University Press, 1988 (in press).

An important forthcoming statement by the founder of deep ecology.

175. **Nash, Roderick. Wilderness and the American Mind, 3rd ed.** New Haven, CT: Yale University Press, 1982. 256 pages.

A penetrating intellectual history of American conservation attitudes, Roderick Nash traces the evolution of wilderness concepts from the Puritan settlers of the New World, to Thoreau, Muir, and Aldo Leopold, to contemporary ecologists. Among the first scholars to apply sociological ideas to conservation history, the text has remained the classic study of wilderness and its role in shaping American consciousness. Extensively documented, a bibliographic essay provides additional information on available resource materials. Environmental history, philosophy.

176. **Nasr, Seyyed Hossein. The Encounter of Man and Nature: The Spiritual Crisis of Modern Man.** London, England: George Allen and Unwin, 1968. 151 pages.

"The thesis presented in this book is simply this: that although science is legitimate in itself, the role and function of science and its application have become illegitimate and even dangerous because of the lack of a higher form of knowledge into which science could be integrated and the destruction of the sacred and spiritual value of nature. To remedy this situation the metaphysical knowledge pertaining to nature must be revived and the sacred quality of nature given back to it once again" (p. 14). Nature cosmology and metaphysics, not recommended for the general reader. Annotated notes.

177. **Nasr, Seyyed Hossein. Knowledge and the Sacred: The Gifford Lectures, 1981.** New York, NY: The Crossroad Publishing Company, 1981. 339 pages.

A corollary to Nasr's earlier *The Encounter of Man and Nature* (1968). In this more recent work, the author continues his study of the sapiential dimensions of human experience, analyzing the process by which the sacred, in the modern world, becomes secularized. In chapter 6, "The Cosmos as Theophany" (pp. 189–220), emphasis is placed on the importance of traditional nature cosmology, where Nasr encounters (in the spiritual experiences of the American Indian, for example) a harmony between divine revelation and natural form. The author sees nature as a primordial source of the sacred realm; its destruction as a symbol of the universal loss of the sacred in modern science and philosophy. Extensive notes.

178. **National Research Council. Ecological Knowledge and Environmental Problem Solving: Concepts and Case Studies.**

Washington, DC: National Academy Press,
1986. 388 pages.

When it comes to applying ecological concepts to specific environmental problems, our appreciation for nature's complexity takes on new and ever greater meaning. Too often we find that ecological "theory" does not adequately align with ecological "fact." This volume attempts to resolve some of the questions surrounding the application of ecological knowledge to environmental problems, outlining a variety of assessment methods for properly doing so. Part I analyzes the various approaches to deciphering ecological information, discussing everything from "stability boundaries" to "population fragmentation." Part II illustrates the application of such knowledge to very real situations—we are given case studies like chapters 17, "Conserving a Regional Spotted Owl Population" (pp. 227–247) and 23, "Ecological Effects of Clearcutting" (pp. 345–357). Primarily for the student of the "environmental sciences," this volume does, however, provide the general reader with invaluable information concerning the role of environmental assessments in monitoring today's conservation practices.

179. Needleman, Jacob. A Sense of the Cosmos:
The Encounter of Ancient Wisdom and
Modern Science. Garden City, NY:
Doubleday, 1975. 178 pages.

Theologian Jacob Needleman believes that the visions of life that come from the religions of Tibet, India, the Middle East, ancient Egypt, and the esoteric knowledge of medieval alchemy and mysticism have enormous implications for redefining our place in the living cosmos. In seven chapters, the author explores such diverse topics as psychotherapy, magic, and the "humanization of truth." Relating these concepts to the religious psychology of modern science and technology, Needleman concludes that today's scientists and technologists operate from a highly egoistic, highly anthropocentric worldview. An excellent introduction to the epistemological relationship between modern science and ancient wisdom.

180. Norton, Byran G., ed. The Preservation of
Species: The Value of Biological Diversity.
Princeton, NJ: Princeton University Press,
1986, 272 pages.

Professor Norton, professor of philosophy at the University of South Florida, has collected a series of essays on the value and preservation of species populations. Section I sketches the magnitude of the present extinction problem; the range of ecological attitudes toward it. Section II, chapters 4 through 8, examines the philosophy and public sentiment concerning biological diversity. The concluding section, chapters 9 through 11, presents three discussions on different aspects of social and biological theory pertaining to environmental management. This section is important because diversity alone, in any given habitat, is not always a natural desideratum and is itself a poor criterion for conservation. The number of species in a habitat tells us very little about that habitat's evolutionary *telos* or *arche*. Ecologists have long been aware of the problems with diversity science and have frequently shown how diversification can (in artificially contrived ecotomes, for example) beget homogenization. Overall, these eleven essays make an important contribution to our present understanding of biological diversity; its role in determining the normative value of biotic communities.

181. **Norton, Bryan G. Why Perserve Natural Variety?** Princeton, NJ: Princeton University Press, 1987. 281 pages.

"If . . . society is to address the entire range of concerns regarding biological diversity," writes the author of this uniquely influential work, "it must reexamine its entire style of life and the values that drive it" (pp. xii). In eleven well-argued chapters, Professor Norton examines the ways in which humans derive values in nature, arguing for a more positive definition of anthropocentric or human-centered approaches.

Methodologically, the author opts for what he calls "transformative values"—values that reinforce an ecological rationale for preserving nonhuman species while simultaneously enhancing the quality of both human and nonhuman life. These transformative values, as defended by Norton, do not occur "intrinsically" in nature, yet discourage purely utilitarian or economic arguments for species preservation. He argues consistently against a purely nonanthropocentric environmental ethic (like Paul Taylor's or David Ehrenfeld's, for example), which, he says, ignores the "character-building" values created by human interaction with the natural world. One might argue that Norton's approach leans toward "strong anthropocentrism"—that "natural objects," in his system can "have value only insofar as they satisfy human demand values" (p.12). But as Norton himself suggests throughout this richly documented work, such an approach may treat nonhuman species as instrumental to human values without making those same values utilitarian or anthropocentric. An important, if not essential, ecophilosophical text. Sponsored by the Center for Philosophy and Public Policy of the University of Maryland. Notes.

182. **Olson, Sigurd F. Sigurd F. Olson's Wilderness Days.** New York, NY: Knopf, 1972. 233 pages.

A bucolic narrative by an infamous naturalist and inhabitant of the Quebitico-Superior lake region. Olson, the author of *The Singing Wilderness*

(1961), describes his experience of the four seasons in this unique and beautiful bioregion. Illustrations, color plates.

183. Ong, Walter J. **Orality and Literacy: The Technologizing of the Word.** New York, NY: Methuen, 1982. 201 pages.

A philosophical anthropology of the oral dimensions of language and literacy. This book should be of important interest to ecophilosophers—Father Ong recognizes crucial existential differences in what he calls primitive (oral) consciousness and textual (chirographic) consciousness. Print or chirographic cultures, asserts the author, "interiorize" consciousness to such a conceptual degree that nature, for all intents and purposes, is eliminated from experience. In a climate where philosophical discourse is itself intricately embedded in print and publishing techniques, we should perhaps reconsider the impact of typography and typographical consciousness on our own definitions and descriptions of nature. (This theme is also addressed in Ivan Illich and Barry Sander's *ABC: The Alphabetization of the Popular Mind*, 1988). Extensive select bibliography.

184. Ophuls, William. **Ecology and the Politics of Scarcity: Prologue to a Political Theory of the Steady State.** San Francisco, CA: W. H. Freeman, 1977. 303 pages.

A three-part critique of American political values and institutions. Ophuls argues, rather convincingly, that unless we change our present political, social, and economic structures, we will be unable to adequately deal with scarce resources. A more organic model of human existence is needed, claims the author, in order to confront the problems of scarcity, environmental pollution, and social disparity. In the second half of the book, Ophuls' organic model is introduced quite less convincingly. The author calls for the creation of a survivalist class of "ecological guardians" to handle the necessary decisions for ecological sanity—even at the expense of social liberties and personal freedom: "The individualistic basis of society, the concept of inalienable rights, the purely self-defined pursuit of happiness, liberty as maximum freedom of action, and *laissez faire* itself all become problematic, requiring major modifications or perhaps even abandonment if we wish to avert inexorable environmental degradation and eventual extinction as a civilization. Certainly, democracy as we know it cannot conceivably survive" (p. 163).

185. Parsons, Howard. **Marx and Engels on Ecology.** Westport, CT: Greenwood Press, 1978. 262 pages.

Howard Parsons, a major interpreter of Marxian thought for American audiences, has selected fifty-nine quotations from the writings of Marx and Engels to illustrate their views on nature, man and nature, man and technology. Along with these quotations, Parsons has assembled a twenty-six page bibliography on relevant ecological literature. All of this is prefaced with a lengthy introduction which outlines the theoretical development of Marxian analysis with respect to its alleged relationship to ecological attitudes. Although Parsons concludes that Marx and Engels "did not anticipate the complex environmental problems that an exponential growth of capitalistic production would bring" (pp. 84–85), he objects to critiques of socialism that suggest it faces the same ecological problems found in capitalist countries.

186. **Partridge, Ernest, ed. Responsibilities to Future Generations: Environmental Ethics.**
Buffalo, NY: Prometheus Books, 1981.
319 pages.

Couched in mostly theological terms, these essays attempt to provide a moral basis for an environmental ethic applicable to both present and future generations. Essays by the editor, Annette Baier, Richard and Val Routley, and several others. The responsibility of humanity to future generations is, as Bryan G. Norton has pointed out, both environmentally and ethically a complex issue. More rigorous and comprehensive analyses than those provided by these essays is needed to resolve the normative problems of temporal distance and ecological axiology.

187. **Passmore, John. Man's Responsibility Toward Nature: Ecological Problems and Western Tradition.** New York, NY: Scribner's, 1974.
213 pages.

The subtitle of Professor Passmore's competent, widely discussed work more correctly identifies its content. The bulk of the volume (Part Two) is devoted to rigorous examinations of four particular ecological problems— "Pollution, Conservation, Preservation, Multiplication." Passmore effectively argues that the basic attitude of the West has not necessarily been environmentally destructive. The history of Western thought and practice is far more complex and should not be stereotyped as such. Any moral conclusions that one draws from Passmore's study must be done so with care, however. Passmore himself offers no cut-and-dried ethical solutions to the West's ecological problems.

188. **Pepper, David. The Roots of Modern Environmentalism.** New Hampshire: Croom Helm, 1984. 246 pages.

A historical and philosophical guide to environmental thought by a Marxist geographer. The longest chapter, "The Marxist Perspective on Nature and Environmentalism," provides a provocative critique of both conventional ecology and the environmental sciences. Pepper's well-documented study takes the United States and Great Britain as prime examples of capitalism at work, while (perhaps uncritically) dismissing the Soviet Union as a poor example of Marxism in practice. Most of Pepper's complaints against American environmental practice/philosophy are informed ones. However, he knows the British environmental literature far better than the American. In sum, a good challenge to conventional wisdom in contemporary ecological thought. Illustrations.

189. **Peters, Richard S. Nature and Conduct.** Royal Institute of Philosophy Lectures, Vol. 8, 1973–74. New York, NY: St. Martin's Press, 1975. 315 pages.

Sixteen lectures on the connection between human conduct and the natural world. Topics include human nature and empirical assumptions in morality, man's relation and attitudes to animals and the environment, ethical issues in cost-benefit analysis and environmental planning, and specific notions such as conscience, needs vs. desires, and roles. Selected lectures include Shirley R. Letwin's "Nature, History, and Morality," John Benson's "Hog in Sloth, Fox in Stealth, Man and Beast in Moral Thinking," Peter Self's "Techniques and Values in Policy Decisions," and John Passmore's well-known "Attitudes in Nature." Passmore's important statement examines the need for what he calls a "new metaphysics," that is, a nonanthropocentric way of thinking about nature and the environment. Other noteworthy entries include those by Ted Henderich, Anthony Quinton, and Richard Hare. Frequent references to Plato, Aristotle, Hume, Kant, Sartre, and Karl Popper. Notes.

190. **Petulla, Joseph M. American Environmentalism: Values, Tactics, Priorities.** College Station: Texas University Press, 1980. 239 pages.

An important work of environmental history emphasizing the value structures of our society and their respective development into ideological traditions. Petulla examines both the emergence of environmental dogmas and the re-establishment of rational environmental principles. Focusing on three traditional schools of environmental thought—the biocentric, ecologic, and economic—the author traces the roles that these as well as opposing positions have played in establishing contemporary environmental policy. A good introductory summary of the major environmental attitudes and their adversary positions. Notes.

191. **Philosophical Inquiry. D. Z. Andriopoulos,**
     Editor. Vol. 8 (Winter/Spring 1986) Nos. 1–2.

This special issue of *Philosophical Inquiry*, an international philosophical quarterly, focuses on the emerging relations between philosophy and ecology. Andrew McLaughlin provides the introduction to this issue, stating that the primary purpose in bringing together these papers "is the hope that more philosophers will turn their skills toward the question posed by the ecological crisis confronting humanity" (p. 2). For McLaughlin, ecology poses a new set of questions for philosophers—questions that perhaps can only be answered by broadening the present scope of epistemological inquiry.

The journal contains eight papers, beginning with Arne Naess' defense of the deep ecology perspective (pp. 10–31). Here Naess further explains the basic principles of deep ecology, clarifying such concepts as "ecosophy T" (self-realization) and "maximum diversity" (maximum symbiosis). The second paper, Hwa Yol Jung's "The Harmony of Man and Nature: A Philosophic Manifesto" (pp. 32–49), reinforces Naess' arguments and at the same time introduces two new terms into the deep ecology lexicon: Sinism and ecopiety. The third selection, by Alan Drengson, offers some general observations on the developmental processes in environmental relations (pp. 50–63). Professor Drengson concludes his paper with a helpful summary on the semantic derivations of ecophilosophical terms.

Following Drengson's is Andrew Brennan's paper, "Ecological Theory and Value in Nature" (pp. 66–89). Brennan wants to broaden the scope of our moral concerns, so "that we come to recognize various natural things as proper objects of moral concern and possessors of moral value" (p. 67). The author points out that deep ecology has generally taken seriously the conceptual foundations of ecological theory. The fifth entry is Ernest Partridge's argument for an "eco-centric" axiology (pp. 96–110). "Does nature, 'by itself,' and/or apart from persons or sentient beings," asks the author, "have any value significance?" Essays by Donald Lee, Richard George, and Robin Attfield conclude the issue, touching on a variety of topics ranging from ethical theory and free enterprise to the possibility of a new environmental ethic in Western tradition.

192. **Pinchot, Gifford. Breaking New Ground.**
     New York, NY: Harcourt, Brace and Co.,
     1947. 522 pages.

Pinchot's autobiography, focusing on the years between 1889 and 1912—the beginnings of American forestry and the conservation of natural resources in the United States. Idiomatic dialogue extracted from Pinchot's diaries, notes, and personal letters.

193. **Prigogine, Ilya, and Stengers, Isabelle. Order Out of Chaos: Man's New Dialogue with Nature.** Boulder, CO: Shambala Publications, 1984. 349 pages.

Models of nature readily change their complexion according to the age of their disclosure. Some models are mechanistic, others organic and personal. In this work, Nobel Laureate Ilya Prigogine and historian of science Isabelle Stengers have constructed a model of nature that reflects a recognizable receptivity to cybernetic principles and theorems. According to the authors, all living things, and many non-living ones, are organized according to "dissipative structures." That is, they maintain and develop their biological identity by (1) monitoring the continual ebb and flow of the energy through their systems, and (2) breaking down other structures' systems in the process of metabolism. The self-organizing "re-adjustment" of the structures' system, however, often causes the entire system to collapse. When that happens, the system reorganizes itself into new dissipative structures with a new "higher" order of complexity and integration; a greater energy flow than its predecessor. Thus, maintain the authors, each successive rendering, because it is more complex than the one preceding it, is even more vulnerable to fluctuations and reordering.

This nonequilibrium conception of nature's metabolic processes suggests that all living systems are fundamentally open and dissipative. The organism-as-process derives its ontological integrity not from its being an integrated, singular thing, but rather from its being a continuously evolving process, whose evolvingness rather than its thingness, is its essence. One of the problems with this conception of nature, and process metaphysics in general, is the promotion of a philosophy of becoming rather than one of being, development rather than form, transformation rather than substance. The temporal desubstantiation of being, ecologically speaking, often promotes an unhealthy disrespect for the integrity of the species form, the "organism-in-itself" is lost in what the authors of this text would call "bifurcated fluctuations" and "energy transformations." Foreword by Alvin Toffler.

194. **Raphael, Ray. Edges: Human Ecology of the Backcountry.** Lincoln, NB: University of Nebraska Press, 1986. 233 pages.

Originally published in 1976, this book "consists of a series of portraits in which the people and places of the Edges are allowed to speak for themselves" (p. 13). The "edges"—the countryside and small towns which cling precariously to rural traditions—embody a human experience rich in tradition and ecological sensibility, asserts the author. Concentrating on the region of northwestern California, Raphael argues for the preservation of the people of the edges; their communities, lifestyles, and truly ecological ways of life.

Applicable to all sparsely populated regions of North America, this study teaches invaluable lessons about the humble dignity of rural life. Includes a new afterword by the author.

195. **Rapoport, Amos. The Meaning of the Built Environment: A Nonverbal Communication Approach.** London, England: Sage Publications, 1982. 224 pages.

Rapoport, one of the founders of the new field of Environment-Behavior Studies, is Distinguished Professor in the School of Architecture and Urban Planning at the University of Wisconsin. In this fascinating work, the author examines the meaning of environment and environmental communication. As the subtitle suggests, the study emphasizes non-linguistic dimensions of the human-nature experience. An important contribution to environmental psychology and ecological architecture. Extensive bibliography.

196. **Rappaport, Roy A. Ecology, Meaning and Religion.** Richmond, CA: North Atlantic Books, 1979. 259 pages.

Seven diverse but not entirely unrelated essays on ecological anthropology. Rappaport, the author of *Pigs for the Ancestors: Ritual in the Ecology of New Guinea* (1968), argues persuasively for the inclusion of the religious consciousness in the anthropological/ecological study of man.

197. **Regan, Tom, and Singer, Peter, eds. Animal Rights and Human Obligations.** Englewood Cliffs, NJ: Prentice-Hall, 1976. 250 pages.

An early collection of essays for and against animal rights. Collected arguments by philosophers and ethologists take positions on a variety of issues: vivisection, vegetarianism, the quantitative or qualitative differences between humans and other animals. Suggested reading list. Appended biographical notes.

198. **Regan, Tom. All That Dwell Therein: Animal Rights and Environmental Ethics.** Berkeley, CA: University of California Press, 1982. 249 pages.

Comprised of ten essays (nine of which have been previously published), this text deals with the issue of human obligations to other animals. Specific topics include vegetarianism, animal experimentation, the normative grounds for an environmental ethic, the ecology of the Native American Indian. On the latter issue, Regan seriously doubts whether we can learn any moral lessons from American Indian culture, criticizing those who try to establish ethical guidelines from romanticized visions of Native American life. Together, the essays are somewhat redundant: the same basic arguments are repeated throughout the work. Regan does provide helpful introductions to the essays which indicate where each essay fits into the development of his thought. Excellent bibliography on animal rights theory.

199. **Regan, Tom. The Case for Animal Rights.**
Berkeley, CA: University of California Press,
1983. 425 pages.

Considered one of the most substantial statements of animal liberation doctrine, *The Case for Animal Rights* presents an exhaustive and systematic argument for the humane treatment of animals. After arguing that animals are not only conscious, but also enjoy a mental life that includes perception, memory, desire, belief, intention, and a sense of the future, Regan sketches out his general ethical theory—what he calls "the rights view." The author supports this normative rights view, however, with an ethics concerning only those "mentally normal mammals of a year or more" (p. 78). Ecophilosophers like J. Baird Callicott have called Regan to task for this rather limited understanding of animal liberation, which prevents harm only to individual members of mammal species rather than a "communities of unfolding organisms." Despite the fact that Regan's case for animal rights is somewhat restricted, its central message is clear and well articulated: "animals have certain basic moral rights and . . . recognition of their rights requires fundamental changes in our treatment of them . . . " (p. xii).

200. **Regan, Tom (Ed.). Earthbound: New Introductory Essays in Environmental Ethics.** New York, NY: Random House, 1984. 371 pages.

While most of these essays are new for the genre of environmental ethics, not all of them are introductory. The editor has invited eight noted philosophers in the field to prepare essays for this volume: subsequently, several of the selections assume too much of the uninitiated reader. This issue is made even more problematic by the fact that the book was designed for an undergraduate audience. The most accessible essays are those by Tom Regan, Mark Sagoff, William Aiken, Alastair Gunn, Kristin Shrader-Frechette, and Edward Johnson. Less accessible are those by Annette Baier, Robert Simon, Dale Jamieson, and Tiber Machan. More monistic than comprehensive, *Earthbound* provides a necessary exploration of several important environmental issues.

201. **Regan, Tom. The Struggle for Animal Rights.**
Clarks Summit, PA: International Society for
Animal Rights, 1987. 197 pages.

A diverse collection of essays by an important figure in the animal rights movement. Regan, whose intellectual work is well known in academic circles, has also put his animal rights philosophy into practice. He has introduced and sponsored animals rights legislation, given testimony before government committees, produced film documentaries, and participated in a number of nonviolent civil disobedience activities. Autobiographical in scope, most of the entries give Regan's own personal reflections on why he is active in the animal rights movement. Several of the essays do give some of Regan's latest thinking on theoretical concerns, including chapters 2, "The Case for Animals Rights" (pp. 44–63) and 8, "The Role of Culture in the Struggle for Animal Rights" (pp. 120–135). Though an informative primer on the animals rights movement in general, the seasoned animal rights philosopher/activist will most likely find the text a remedial one.

202. **Reinhart, Peter, ed. To Be Christian Is to Be Ecologist.** Epiphany, Vol. 6, No. 1. San Francisco, CA: Epiphany Press, 1985. 116 pages.

A collection of essays arguing for the need of Christian men and women to feel deeply religious about nature. The editor believes that the Christian community has enormous potential for resolving the present environmental crisis, that Christianity is just beginning to take moral responsibility for the ecological plight of the earth. Many scholars have blamed the "otherworldliness" of Christianity for our present environmental problems; however, as Reinhart and the other authors of this monograph argue, it may well be the authentic return of Christian stewardship practice that preserves nature. Discussions on biblical interpretation, spirituality, grace, and stewardship.

203. **Richardson, Robert D. Henry Thoreau: A Life of the Mind.** Berkeley, CA: University of California Press, 1986. 455 pages.

For ecophilosophy the transcendentalist tradition is an important one: both Emerson and Thoreau provide rich intellectual frameworks for contemporary ecological thought and practice. Meticulously documented, this biographical study brings to bear many new insights into the life of Thoreau as well as the transcendentalist tradition his work embodies. In chronological sequence the author recounts the life of Thoreau from 1837 when he was twenty, to his death at age forty-five in 1862. We are told of Thoreau's exposure to a number of philosophical systems (including Stoicism and Hindu Idealism), as well as to the writings of William Blake, Goethe, Amos Alcott and, of course, Ralph Waldo Emerson. Also, Richardson is careful to define Thoreau's intellectual education in the context of his vast experience of nature and natural phenonemena. For Thoreau, it appears the "life of letters" and the "life of a naturalist" were completely complementary ones. He could read Aristotle as comfortably as he could a spring thaw, and the reading of one would greatly enhance the reading of the other. In this respect, Thoreau was perhaps our first ecophilosopher. Extensive notes.

204. **Rifkin, Jeremy, with Howard, Ted. The Emerging Order: God in the Age of Scarcity.** New York, NY: Ballantine, 1979. 285 pages.

A critique of the liberal ethos and the "age of expansion," the authors acknowledge the very real and present possibility of a Christian "conservation ethic." Provides a somewhat superficial history of modern liberalism, but offers a more penetrating historical analysis of American Evangelical and Charismatic movements. A watershed book for those interested in the ecopolitical, ecotheological aspects of Christian stewardship doctrine. Notes.

205. **Rifkin, Jeremy, with Howard, Ted. Entropy: A New World View.** New York, NY: Viking, 1980. 305 pages.

The Second Law of Thermodynamics—the Entropy Law—states that all energy flows inexorably from the usable to the unusable and from the orderly to the disorderly. The Entropy Law also suggests that time, as we experience it, is an irreversible forward process. "Time only goes in one direction, and that is forward. That forward direction, in turn, is a function of the change in entropy. Time reflects the change in energy from concentration to diffusion or from order to increasing disorder" (p.47).

Furthering the application of the Entropy Law to less metaphysical areas of inquiry, Rifkin applies the principles of the second law to education, urbanization, agriculture, health, economics, and politics. The author maintains that the Entropy Law can explain why science and technology do not provide the benefits they perennially promise; namely, growth and progress. Generally, the application of natural law to human and social experience is doomed from the onset. Rifkin, however, provides the reader with more than an iron-clad, all-embracing law of nature—his vision of a society living within the boundaries of thermodynamic theorems is more heuristic than governing. Notes and extensive bibliography.

206. **Rifkin, Jeremy. Algeny.** New York: Viking Press, 1983. 298 pages.

Algeny—the genetic manipulation and development of species to conform to human purposes and desires—is a neologism first coined by Joshua Lederberg, president of Rockefeller University. In this important book, Mr. Rifkin critically examines algeny, the coming age of biotechnology, our relationship to nature, the myths and mythology of Darwinian science. The author warns that an algeny-type future might be suicidal for humanity: he opts for a more ecologically sensitive paradigm: "Two futures beckon us. We can choose to engineer the life of the planet, creating a second nature in our own image, or we can choose to participate with the rest of the living kingdom. . . . Our choice, in the final analysis, depends on what we value most in life. If it is physical security, perpetuation at all costs, that we value most, then technological mastery over the becoming process brings with it a price far greater than any humanity has ever had to contend with. By choosing the power of authorship, humanity gives up, once and for all, the most precious gift of all, companionship" (p. 252). Notes.

207. **Rifkin, Jeremy. Declaration of a Heretic.**
Boston and London, England: Routledge & Kegan Paul, 1985. 140 pages.

Jeremy Rifkin, a social scientist, author and activist, directs the Foundation on Economic Trends in Washington, D.C. Devoting over a decade to the study and critique of science, technology, and ethics, the author is perhaps best known for his legal battles against the unrestrained use of genetic engineering technologies. His lawsuits against the National Institutes of Health, Department of Defense, and the United States Department of Agriculture have received worldwide attention. In *Declaration of a Heretic*, Rifkin attempts to present his own unique view of the nature of progress, the appropriate forms of social organization, and the legitimate uses of technology. He adamantly defends his own "heretical" ecophilosophical position by compassionately describing the worldview which informs his own alternative vision of the future.

The text is divided into three parts; the first two sections consisting of critiques of the nuclear worldview and genetic engineering respectively, while the last part deals primarily with "empathetic" alternatives to these worldviews. Contains a comprehensive reading list, categorized under the following headings: "Critique of the Modern World View," "Alternative Philosophies and Epistemologies," "Critical and Empathetic Science," "Imaginative Cognition," "Religion and Spirituality," "Alternative Psychologies," "Holistic Health," "Education for Human Development," "Economics, Politics, Culture and a New World Order," "New Agriculture and Animal Husbandry," "Business and the Workplace," "Ecology and Environmentalism," and "Shelter."

208. **Rifkin, Jeremy. Time Wars: The Primary Conflict in Human History.** New York, NY: Henry Holt, 1987. 263 pages.

A chronosophic analysis of the temporal dimensions of human experience—past, present, and future. The author analyzes the time dimension of both traditional and modern cultures while also examining the latest information about biological clocks and computer simulation. "The new computer technology" writes Rifkin, "is already changing the way we conceptualize time and, in the process, is changing the way we think about ourselves and the world around us. We are entering a new time zone radically different from anything we have experienced in the past. So different is the new computer time technology that it is creating the context for the emergence of a new language of the mind and an altered state of consciousness, just as the automated clock did in the thirteenth century when it laid open the door to the Age of Mechanism and the specter of a clockwork universe" (p. 13). Extensive notes and select bibliography.

209. **Rolston, Holmes, III. Philosophy Gone Wild.**
Buffalo, NY: Prometheus, 1986. 269 pages.

A collection of fifteen previously published articles by the associate editor of *Environmental Ethics*, *Philosophy Gone Wild* is a major statement about the ethics of environmental concerns. Professor Rolston, who also teaches at Colorado State University, writes with the sensitivity of a naturalist and with the depth and rigor of an accomplished philosopher. In summarizing this work one could say that although Rolston tackles the questions of science, religion and values in nature equally well; he tends to focus his efforts on the theme of natural values, their relationship to veridical experience in nature. The articles are arranged in four overlapping and related sections: "Ethics and Nature," "Values in Nature," "Environmental Philosophy and Practice," and "Nature in Experience." Over the past decade, Rolston's work has been partly responsible for the recent "environmental turn" in philosophical literature—this carefully arranged compilation of his work illustrates why.

210. **Rolston, Holmes, III. Environmental Ethics:**
Duties to and Values in the Natural World.
Philadelphia, PA: Temple University Press,
1988. 391 pages.

A systemic, cross-disciplinary philosophy of nature. As in his earlier work, the author presents an analysis of natural values as mediated by human interests. Rolston's environmental ethic rests entirely on humanity's valuational indebtedness to the natural world. Nature, because it contributes positively to human experience, must be preserved because of its capacity to enhance, sustain, or even make possible, human life. According to the author, values are "carried" by nature in both objective and assigned ways: Nature may have historical value, economic value, scientific value, recreational value, or even religious value. It is these values which determine our duties to nature, and each must be analyzed with respect to their axiological relationship to human experience

Rolston avoids anthropocentricism here by grounding human experience in ecological events: humans cannot be substantively removed from nature and therefore one may derive moral duties in it. The result is an ethical pluralism much like Christopher Stone's in which plants, animals, or ecosystems are graded hierarchically according to their intrinsic/instrumental worth to the larger community. Our duties to the natural world include following these valuational agencies, so that human life and the life of the biosphere may be dialectically brought together. A major effort by a leading ecophilosopher. Contents include: "Humans Valuing the Natural Environment" (pp. 1–44); "Higher Animals: Duties to Sentient Life" (pp. 45–93); "Organisms: Duties to Organic Life" (pp. 94–125); "Life in Jeopardy: Duties to Endangered Species" (pp. 126–159); "Life in Community: Duties to Ecosystems" (pp. 160–191); "The Concept of Natural Value: A Theory for Environmental Ethics" (pp. 192–245); "Environmental Policy: An Ethic of the Commons" (pp. 246–289); "Environmental Business: An Ethic for Commerce" (pp. 290–327); "Down to Earth: Persons in Natural History" (pp. 328–354). Notes. Selected bibliography.

211. Roszak, Theodore. **Where the Wasteland Ends: Politics and Transcendence in Postindustrial Society.** Garden City, NY: Anchor/Doubleday, 1973. 492 pages.

An exhaustive and well-known examination of the ways in which certain dimensions of the human personality have been denatured in Western culture over the past several hundred years. The author argues that this process of desacralization, through the repression of religious sensibilities, has led to the creation of unnatural simulated environments; technocratic institutions that foster psychic alienation and personal despair. The wasteland of urban-industrial development, argues Roszak, has replaced the sacramental vision of religious worldviews with a single vision of a totally scientized culture.

Contents include thirteen well-articulated chapters arranged in three parts. Part One, "The Wasteland Within and About Us," tells "how the urban-industrial revolution generated an artificial environment, and what style of politics and consciousness has followed from that environment" (p. 1). Part Two, "Single Vision and Newton's Sleep," examines "how the psychology of single vision, beginning as a defense of the sacred, was carried by Christianity into the Scientific Revolution, and how an alienated natural philosophy, after achieving cultural supremacy in the modern world, has betrayed its brightest ideals" (p. 107). And lastly, Part Three, "A Politics of Eternity," looks at "how the Romantic artists, dissenting from single vision, rediscovered the meaning of the transcendent symbols and thereby returned Western culture to the Old Gnosis, and what part the ideal of rhapsodic intellect must play in our journey to the visionary commonwealth" (p. 275). Extensive notes.

212. **Roszak, Theodore. Person/Planet: The Creative Disintegration of Industrial Society.** Garden City, NY: Anchor/Doubleday, 1978. 347 pages.

"This book concerns itself with the point at which human psychology and natural ecology meet. [Roszak's] purpose is to suggest that the environmental anguish of the earth has entered our lives as a radical transformation of human identity. The needs of the planet and the needs of the person have become one, and together they have begun to act upon the central institutions of our society with a force that is profoundly subversive, but which carries within it the promise of cultural renewal" (p. xix). Roszak concludes this text on psychological and ecological reform with chapters addressing both the responsibility of intellectuals in preserving rural culture and the issue of human-scale and urbanization in creating sustainable economic practices. Notes.

213. **Rouner, Leroy S. On Nature.** Notre Dame, IN: University of Notre Dame Press, 1984. 188 pages.

Volume six in a series of publications by Boston University's Institute for Studies in Philosophy and Religion—an interdisciplinary and ecumenical forum that, according to the editor, "does not represent any philosophical school or religious tradition" (p. vii). The text is divided into three well-defined parts: "Natural Science and the Philosophy of Nature," "Nature in Cross-Cultural Perspective," and "Human Nature in the Natural World." Each third is further divided into fourths with essays by leading scholars from their respective fields: W. V. Quine, Stephen Toulmin, Huston Smith, Charles Hartshorne, Lynn Margulis, Jurgen Moltmann, etc. The eleven essays are prefaced with an informative and explicatory introduction by the editor, Leroy Rouner, who also serves as the institute's director. Bibliographical notes on contributors. Philosophy of nature. Nature and religious aspects.

214. **Sagoff, Mark. The Economy of Earth: Philosophy, Law, and the Environment.** Cambridge, MA: Cambridge University Press. (forthcoming).

215. **Sale, Kirpatrick. Human Scale.** New York, NY: Coward, McCann & Geoghegan, 1980. 558 pages.

Arguing that "small is beautiful" and "bigger" is not necessarily "better," social commentator Kirpatrick Sale examines the ways in which scale affects our social, economic, and political realities. Sale sees the recovery of "human scale" in our institutions as a cultural, psychological, and ecological imperative. A heavily researched and well-documented book.

216. **Sale, Kirpatrick. Dwellers in the Land: The Bioregional Vision.** San Francisco, CA: Sierra Club Books, 1985. 217 pages.

Bioregionalism is a term first propagated by writer Peter Berg and ecologist Raymond Dasmann more than a decade ago. It implies the existence of very real boundaries in the environment which define and promote particular categories of human and social experience. Recently, the bioregional philosophy has become influential in shaping a great deal of ecological thought, envisioning a world based not on arbitrary political borders, but on natural geographic regions defined by particular flora, fauna, landforms, and watersheds.

Sale's articulation of the concept in this work—how bioregional philosophy encourages us to be "dwellers in the land" rather than despots over nature—is to be commended. It is difficult, however, to comprehend the "when and how" of Sale's intended implementation of this regionalist idea. His tone speaks of urgency, yet he insists that his regional separatism is a gradual process: "[Bioregionalism] suggests that the processes of change—first of organizing, educating, activating a constituency, and then of reimagining, reshaping, and recreating a continent—are slow, steady, continuous, and methodical, not revolutionary and cataclysmic. . . . The bioregional project has to be an evolutionary one. It is only by a long and regular process of awakening, education, study, revision, faith, and experimentation that people will ease themselves into such a society" (p. 176–177).

Sale insists that bioregionalism should develop organically out of the ecological context of human/nature interaction, yet he fails to acknowledge that his "bioregional imperative" predescribes those very boundaries. He says that bioregional politics should be decentralized politics, yet argues that bioregionalism does not "envision a takeover of the national government or a vast rearrangement of the national machinery" (p. 170). Full of such contradictions, *Dwellers in the Land* serves better as a primer on bioregional philosophy and its development than as a manifesto of a possible human ecology in harmony with nature.

217. **Satin, Mark. New Age Politics: Healing Self and Society.** New York, NY: Delta Books, 1979. 349 pages.

According to the author, "New Age Politics" recognizes the correlation between the attitudes and consciousness of individuals and the quality of social institutions they foster. The new politics is a healing politics, embracing the spiritual, human-potential, feminist, environmental, and appropriate technology movements under a broad political umbrella. Since the book's publication some nine years ago, what the New Age movement has become remains unclear. Many of the groups cited in the text no longer share or reflect deep, alternative, ecological, or voluntary simplicity lifestyles. They are rapidly becoming an integral part of the technocratic industrial complex they once rejected. In fact, technology, in the hand of most New Age thinkers is viewed as a potentially liberating, intrinsically beneficial "force." Despite obvious deficiencies in this early attempt to philosophically define the parameters of a radical alternative political platform, Satin does give us an insightful critique of the modern liberal ethos: the old liberal mythology that encourages the "economics of oppression" and the domination of nature. Contains an extensive resource section listing 270 books, 50 periodicals, and 100 New Age-oriented groups.

218. **Schaeffer, Francis. Pollution and the Death of Man: The Christian View of Ecology.**
Wheaton, IL: Tyndale House, 1970. 125 pages.

The role of Christianity in promoting human estrangement and alienation from nature is a hotly debated topic among environmental theologians and philosophers. Over the past several decades Christianity has received an enormous amount of press as to its proper historical role in shaping environmental awareness. Christian principles remain, even today, strong in the environmental movement.

In *Pollution and the Death of Man*, Francis Schaeffer, a well-known Christian theologian, presents his own "Christian view of ecology." The book's five essays maintain that the biblical tradition has much to say about the proper care of the earth and its inhabitants. Schaeffer's position, because it attacks pantheism and embraces the so-called human-centered stewardship position (that humans are the ultimate beneficiaries of nature), has been criticized as being anthropocentric by some ecophilosophers. Schaeffer, in the essay "No More than the Grass" (pp. 17–33), counters this charge by saying that purely pantheistic (read: biocentric) nature philosophies are uncritically anti-human: they "always bring man to an impersonal and low place rather than elevating him. . . . Those who propose the pantheistic answer ignore this fact—that far from raising nature to man's height, pantheism must push both man and nature down into a bog. . . . Pantheism leaves us with the Marquis de Sade's dictum, 'What is right, is right,' in morals, and man becomes no more than the grass" (pp. 32, 33). Appendix. Christian stewardship. Ecotheology.

219. **Scheler, Max. Man's Place in Nature.**
Translation by Hans Meyerhoff. New York,
NY: Farrar, Straus & Giroux, 1961. 105 pages.

One of the founders of the philosophical movement known as
phenomenology, Max Scheler's philosophical anthropology has made many
noteworthy contributions to both the human and social sciences, contributing important ethical, religious, psychological, and social ideas to the study
of human existence. At the end of his life, Scheler assigned to philosophy the
broad task of studying mankind in relation to his biological, psychological,
ideological, and social developments. This work is such a study.

Written with the knowledge of his impending death, the text is an impressive although unfinished work of important ecophilosophical significance.
Part One, "The Stages of Psychological Life in Plant, Animal, and Man" (pp.
8–34), summarizes Scheler's "hierarchy" of psychic and biotic experience,
beginning with plant life and ending with humans. In this selection, Scheler
poses to the reader, the following question: To what degree is man different
from the natural world? Scheler's rather idealistic answer to this metaphysical question appears at first to place the "essence" of man over that of the
natural world. However, Scheler ultimately argues, in this and subsequent
essays, that a psychophysical unity of human and nature—a view of human
consciousness and spirit submerged organically in the biological lifeworld—most accurately describes the ontological place of man in nature.
This edition, originally published in 1928 as *Die Stellung des Menschen im
Kosmos*, offers one of the better translations of this sometimes complex and
difficult work. Introduction by Hans Meyerhoff.

220. **Scherer, Donald, and Attig, Thomas. eds.**
Ethics and the Environment. Englewood
Cliffs, NJ: Prentice-Hall, 1983. 236 pages.

A collection of twenty, mostly philosophical essays on environmental
ethics by leading spokespersons in the field. Most of the articles (all but two)
have appeared elsewhere, but all have been edited for republication in this
particular volume. Divided into two major parts, the nine papers comprising
Part One, "Defining an Environmental Ethic," address the conceptual issue
of whether or not environmental ethics is a part of, or distinct from, traditional ethical discourses and principles (Papers by Aldo Leopold, W. H. Murdy,
Mark Sagoff, Kenneth E. Goodpaster, Holmes Rolston, III, J. Baird Callicott,
Donald Scherer, and John Rodman). Part Two, "Specific Environmental
Problems," addresses more applied and practical issues like land-use and
property rights; the use of cost-benefit analyses for determining environmental policy. (Papers by Eugene C. Hargrove, Philip Soper, Chief Justice Hal-
lows, Alasdair MacIntyre, Robert C. Socolow, Alan Gewirth, Ralph B. Potter,

William T. Blackstone, Donald Scherer, Thomas Schelling, and Mark Sagoff.) An excellent anthology. Select bibliography.

221. **Schmookler, Andrew Bard. The Parable of the Tribes: The Problem of Power in Social Evolution.** Boston, MA: Houghton Mifflin Company, 1984. 400 pages.

An ambitious, cross-disciplinary study devoted to analyzing social evolution from primitive to modern times. The "parable of the tribes" refers to the inevitability of any given society to "invest" its members in the struggle for power and social dominance. According to Schmookler, this investment cannot be politically avoided because power begets power: once competition is introduced into a social system, there is no escaping its totalizing effects. Chapters 6 and 7 (Book II, pp. 215–330) should be of greatest interest to ecophilosophers, as the relationship of man to nature is discussed in the context of bodily, ecological, social, and economic "systems." Notes, bibliography.

222. **Schneider, Stephen H., and Morton, Lynne. The Primordial Bond: Exploring Connections between Man and Nature through the Humanities and Sciences.** New York, NY: Plenum Press, 1981. 324 pages.

The authors, one a climatologist, the other in the humanities, present a creative and non-technical version of humans' embeddedness in nature. One of the most creative aspects of the book is its use of photographs and graphics to illustrate the ecological inclinations of various social periods and societies. The greatest portion of the book, however, concerns the concept of natural cycles as a pattern that connects man to nature, the sciences to the humanities. Chapter 3, "Humanistic Expressions of Cycles in Nature" (pp. 43–73), suggests that man's primordial bond is indeed a cyclical bond. This view is reinforced with many references to cycles in various cultures, from the cyclical cosmologies of the pre-Socratics, to psychological speculations about the collective unconscious. The authors conclude that by recognizing and respecting cycles in nature, humanity can begin to enjoy a more harmonious ecological relationship to the natural world.

223. **Schultz, R. C., and Hughes, J. D., eds. Ecological Consciousness. Essays from the Earthday X Colloquium, University of Denver, April 21–24, 1980.** Washington, D.C.: University Press of America, 1981. 488 pages.

This collection of 19 papers provides a good introductory cross section of the literature and its fundamental tenets. Representing a broad range of disciplines, methodologies, and literary styles, this eclectic assortment of environmental ideologies ends with a valuable bibliographic essay by deep ecologist George Sessions. Sessions' bibliographic survey provides excellent background material to the various philosophical strands weaving together the environmental philosophy movement and concludes this volume nicely. Representative essays by Dolores LaChapelle, Ernest Patridge, Holmes Rolston, III, Schultz and Hughes, Edward Kormandy, and Calvin Martin.

224. **Schumacher, E. F. Small Is Beautiful: Economics as if People Mattered.** New York, NY: Harper & Row, 1973. 290 pages.

A broad critique of the intentions and technology fueling the modern economic machine. Schumacher argues for the implementation of small, human-scale technology—what Schumacher has called "technology with a human face" (pp. 138–151). Contains his widely circulated essay "Buddhist Economics" (pp. 50–58) which views the production of local resources for local needs as the "most rational way of economic life" (p. 55). Introduction by Theodore Roszak. Notes.

225. **Schumacher, E. F. A Guide for the Perplexed.** New York, NY: Harper & Row, 1977. 147 pages.

A philosophical guidebook for personal and spiritual survival in the modern (unecological) world. Presents a defense of the indispensability of religion and religious frameworks of human organization. Repudiates scientism, hierarchical modes of thinking, and the "cult of the self." Notes.

226. **Schwartz, William, ed. Voices for the Wilderness.** New York, NY: Ballantine, 1969. 366 pages.

The preservation of wilderness and wilderness areas is a topical issue for ecophilosophers. Contemporary ecophilosophy owes a great deal to those voices who have sung the praises of unspoiled and untamed wilderness— John Muir, Aldo Leopold, Henry David Thoreau, John Burroughs, Joseph Wood Krutch, and Sigurd Olson, to mention only a few. *Voices for the Wilderness*, an anthology of thirty-two short vignettes on wilderness issues and topics, provides both old and new arguments for the preservation of our wilderness areas. Selected essays by David Brower, A. Starker Leopold, Paul Brooks, Ashley Montagu, Sigurd Olson, Joseph Wood Krutch, Frank Darling and Paul Sears. Arranged under the headings, "The Problem of Wilderness Preservation," "The Values that Wilderness Preservation Seeks to

Preserve," and "The Program and Outlook for Wilderness Preservation." All essays have appeared previously in other sources.

227. **Seamon, David, and Mugerauer, Robert, eds.**
Dwelling, Place, and Environment: Towards
a Phenomenology of Person and World.
Dordrecht, The Netherlands: Martinus
Nijhoff Publishers, 1985. 310 pages.

A four-part volume of seventeen essays outlining an ecophenomenology of person, place, and environment. Heavily influenced by the writings of philosopher Martin Heidegger, this anthology stresses the importance of structuring our lived environments according to principles uncovered experientially in nature.

Part I contains two excellent essays: one by Robert Mugerauer, "Language and the Emergence of the Environment" (pp. 51–70); the other by Joseph Grange, "Place, Body and Situation" (pp. 71–86). Mugerauer's essay is unique in that he emphasizes the role of language in articulating environmental epistemes; he sees language as structured by both word *and* world. Part II, "Environment and Place," extends the discussions found in the previous section, giving further arguments for the role of environmental experience in shaping human reality. Part III, a four-essay section entitled "Place and Dwelling," turns directly to the question of living-in-place; each author asks how we, as seekers of right-livelihood, might best dwell on the earth. "Discovering Wholes," the last and final section, attempts to identify unifying themes and structures in ecophenomenological anaysis, suggesting that because of nature's complexity, specific environmental experiences must be understood in relationship to essential and greater wholes. Notes.

228. **Serpell, James. In the Company of Animals:**
A Study of Human-Animal Relationships.
New York, NY: Basil Blackwell, 1986.
215 pages.

Serpell, a research associate in animal behavior at the University of Cambridge, studies the contributions of animals and pets to human health and welfare. In both modern times and in history, notes Serpell, the pet has played an important role in breaking the barriers between humans and nature. Historically, animal-human relations are of greater importance than one might imagine: we do indeed need to rethink the history of humanity as it evolved in its relationship to other animals. *In Company of Animals* is a well-documented study, full of cross-cultural anecdotes and historical data. Animal rights and welfare. Notes.

229. **Shepard, Paul, and McKinley, Daniel, eds.**
The Subversive Science: Essays Toward an
Ecology of Man. Boston, MA: Houghton,
1969. 453 pages.

This textbook-styled anthology presents a thoughtful evaluation of the ecology of human populations by students of biology, ecology, sociology, anthropology, and architecture. An excellent five-part primer of human ecology, and environmental and ecological ethics. Introduction by Paul Shepard.

230. **Shepard, Paul. The Tender Carnivore and the**
Sacred Game. New York, NY: Scribners, 1973.
302 pages.

An ecotopian vision that generally (and sometimes naively) seeks the return of man the hunter/gatherer. Shepard's genetic reductionism maintains that the human species is designed for a non-agriculture existence: he condemns farming as a corrupting concept, responsible for the "ten thousand year environmental crisis." In the concluding section, Shephard presents his recipe for ecological utopia and proposes a "cynegetic society"—a future in which cities of no more than 150,000 people are located on continental perimeters. Excellent select bibliography. Illustrations by Fons Van Woerkom.

231. **Shepard, Paul. Thinking Animals: Animals**
and the Development of Human
Intelligence. New York, NY: Viking Press,
1978. 274 pages.

A precursor to *Nature and Madness* (1982), human ecologist Paul Shepard argues in this earlier work that the psychological development of our consciousness is integrally involved with other animals. The learning processes of our children, says the author, are dependent upon the existence of other animal species. Supporting his thesis with examples from mythology, literature, anthropology, and human behavior, the author contends that because animals figure so strongly in our dreams, works of art, our speech, and our images—in the very core of the human imagination—we have a very real psychological need for natural, animal rich, ecosystems.

232. **Shepard, Paul. Nature and Madness.** San
Francisco, CA: Sierra Club Books, 1982.
178 pages.

The author of the work borrows models from developmental psychology in order to better articulate the connection between human maturation and environmental degradation. Shepard's analysis is a cross-cultural one, he has chosen four distinct periods of human history in which to examine the developmental stages of personhood: (1) the domesticators of earliest agriculture (pp. 12–46), (2) the era of the desert fathers (pp. 47–74), (3) the Reformation (pp. 75–92), and (4) the present day industrial society (pp. 93–108). Shepard suggests that individuals of contemporary Western cultures remain, all their lives, in a stage of early adolescence. A phase, he says, marked by intense emotions and infantile behavior. Shepard concludes that many environmental problems could be avoided if people were to realize their natural ontogenies; i.e., develop into a full adulthood of responsible maturity. Extensive notes.

233. **Shi, David E. Plain Living and High Thinking in American Culture.** New York, NY: Oxford University Press, 1985. 332 pages.

The idea of "plain living and high thinking" has been a recurring theme in American life and thought. In this learned study, the author draws from a variety of original sources, illustrating the complex relationship between virtuous ideas and practical, self-sufficient lifestyles. Chapters on the ideas and activities of the Puritans, Quakers, and early Republicans, as well as ones addressing the influence of simple living philosophy on the contemporary era. (See chapter 10, "Affluence and Anxiety," pp. 248–276). For those seeking better historical and social ground in which to sow the modern ecological sensibility, this is an invaluable text. Epilogue. Notes.

234. **Shi, David E. In Search of the Simple Life.** Salt Lake City, UT: Gibbs M. Smith, 1986. 345 pages.

Simplicity is an old and universal ethic. In America, John Winthrop, Thomas Jefferson, Ralph Waldo Emerson, Thoreau and John Burroughs have all expounded on the virtues of the plain and simple life. Indeed, as Shi remarks in the introduction to this remarkable anthology, "the concept of simpler living has always been a prominent aspect of American thought" (p. 3). Collected here, in one volume, are over 100 selections from original American sources: from the lesser known writings of Caroline Kirkland, author of *Forest Life* (1842); John Woolman, the eighteenth century preacher; and the Southern Agrarians (*I'll Take My Stand*, 1930), to the better-known works of Lewis Mumford, Gary Snyder, and Wendell Berry. "Ecological Simplicity," the ninth and final chapter of the book (pp. 295–332), focuses directly on ecological matters, though nearly every chapter contains wisdom applicable to ecological ideals and principles. Each chapter is prefaced by substantial introductions; headnotes provide background and context for most selections. An important sourcebook for those wanting a better understanding of simple living advocates and the ecological ideas they espoused. Photographs, illustrations, select bibliography.

235. **Shrader-Frechette, K. S. Environmental Ethics.** Pacific Grove, CA: Boxwood Press, 1981. 358 pages.

Comprised of twenty-five readings, in a dozen self-contained chapters, *Environmental Ethics* serves as a timely introduction to moral philosophy and environmental issues. Essays by the editor, Nathan Hare, Garrett Hardin, Daniel Callahan, H. F. Kraybill, Bernard Cohen, Ralph Nader, W. C. Wagner, and W. H. Davis. Designed, for the general reader. Notes, bibliography.

236. **Singer, Peter. Animal Liberation: A New Ethics for Our Treatment of Animals.** New York, NY: The New Review, 1975. 297 pages.

Singer's book focuses primarily on two main issues: the raising of animals for food and the use of animals for scientific experimentation. Contains Singer's well-known arguments against "speciesism," the "prejudice or attitude of bias toward the interests of members of one's own species and against those of members of other species" (p. 7). Appendixes: "Cooking for Liberated People," "Further Reading," and "Organizations."

237. **Singer, Peter. The Expanding Circle: Ethics and Sociobiology.** New York, NY: Farrar, Straus and Giroux, 1981. 190 pages.

In this work, sociobiology, a science which some say has more to say about ethics than philosophy does, is favorably critiqued by philosopher Peter Singer. The basic problem, given the assumptions of evolution, says the author, is to expand the boundaries of altruism to include all sentient life. To do so, however, requires less of a biological solution (like E. O. Wilson's) than one based on reason. Although Singer's altruistic rationality *is* considered a product of our biology, he denies, in the final analysis, the use of biological principles to guide our ethical concerns (So where is the sociobiology?). Although many will find the work an important one, the text says little about how we might *concretely* apply sociobiological principles to everyday environmental concerns.

238. **Siu, R. G. H. The Tao of Science: An Essay on Western Knowledge and Eastern Wisdom.** Cambridge, MA: MIT Press, 1957. 180 pages.

A critique of Western science and reason and its application to the humanities, education, and corporate America. Provides alternative, Eastern philosophical approaches to knowledge and our understanding of nature.

239. **Skolimowski, Henryk. Eco-Philosophy:**
Designing New Tactics for Living. London
and New Hampshire: Marion Boyars, 1981.
117 pages.

Henryk Skolimowski, a professor of philosophy at the University of
Michigan (Department of Humanities, College of Engineering), has written
extensively on the history of science and technology and is today considered
a leading ecophilosopher. He has established ecophilosophy centers in Ann
Arbor, Michigan, and in London and is also the associate editor of the journal *The Ecologist*. In this small but important book, the author calls for a
return to an ecological humanism, a new conception of human values in
which "the philosophy of man and the philosophy of nature are aspects of
each other" (p. 53).

The opening chapters of the text provide historical and conceptual critiques of Western philosophy, the scientific worldview, and center particularly around the question of knowledge and values in Western epistemology. In
the remaining three chapters Skolimowski outlines, in greater detail, his
ecological humanistic vision, placing noticeable emphasis on the transformational metaphysics of Christian theologian Teilhard de Chardin.

Because Skolimowski believes that a Teilhardian-styled stewardship
practice would allow for the "creative transformation" of the nonhuman
world by man, his ecological ethics has been labeled by some
ecophilosophers as unapologetically anthropocentric. Skolimowski counters
this charge in this and later discussions by stating that while it is right to fight
against the limitations and dangers of anthropocentrism in ecological
thought, his ecological ethics is neither anthropocentric nor overtly human-
centered (in the traditional philosophical sense). In the end, says
Skolimowski, there is only the *human* point of view, and we humans must
work together—regardless of our autological assumptions—to preserve the
life on this planet.

240. **Skolimowski, Henryk. Eco-Theology: Toward**
a Religion of Our Times. Ann Arbor, MI:
Eco-philosophy Publications No. 2, 1985.
64 pages.

A small booklet exploring the author's version of ecological theology, the
importance of reverential thinking in ecological thought, the religious
psychology of Western religious practice.

241. **Snyder, Gary. Turtle Island.** New York, NY:
New Directions, 1974. 114 pages.

Winner of the Pulitzer Prize for poetry, *Turtle Island* is a collection of
poems and essays which weave together a variety of old and new ecological

perceptions. According to eco-poet Snyder, Turtle Island is "the old/new name for the continent, based on many creation myths of the people who have been living here for millennia, and reapplied by some of them to 'North America' in recent years" (Introductory Note). Also contains the author's thoughts on the relationship of Buddhist philosophy to ecological ideas and sensibilities.

242. **Snyder, Gary. The Old Ways: Six Essays.**
San Francisco, CA: City Light Books, 1977.
96 pages.

Six essays dedicated to the memory of philosopher Alan Watts, *The Old Ways* is a book about the ecological wisdom of the ancients, to be recaptured, "forever new."

243. **Snyder, Gary. The Real Work: Interviews and Talks, 1964–1979.** New York, NY: New Directions, 1980. 189 pages.

A generous sampling of Gary Snyder's most interesting interviews and lectures—many reprinted from otherwise obscure and inaccessible sources. Discussions on Buddhism, American Indians, myths, ecology, human consciousness, and Snyder's own biographical history. The interviewers include Dom Aeired Graham, Peter Barry Chowka, and Nathaniel Tarn. Edited, with an introduction by William Scott McLean. Appendix.

244. **Spretnak, Charlene. The Spiritual Dimension of Green Politics.** Santa Fe, NM: Bear & Company, 1986. 95 pages.

The place of spirituality in ecological practices and Green party platforms has become a much debated topic in North American Green circles. Some see the deepest sources of Green principles as spiritual ones, others see the spiritual dimension as irrelevant to the advancement of a Green *realpolitik*. To be sure, the question is a difficult one. This slender volume attempts to initiate discussion on the issue with Spretnak defending a synthesis of both Green and religious values. The question is left open to how much religious content should be addressed in Green meetings and publications, but the overall message is that the Green movement can no longer afford to ignore the spiritual values guiding political practice. Appendix: "Ten Key Values of the American Green Movement" (pp.76–82).

245. **Spring, David and Eileen, eds. Ecology and Religion in History.** New York, NY: Harper & Row, 1974. 154 pages.

A collection of seven reprinted although celebrated essays on the religious background of the present environmental crisis. Selections by Lynn White, John Macquarrie, James Barr, Lewis Moncrief, Yi-Fu Tuan, René Dubos, and Arnold Toynbee.

246. **Squires, Edwin R., ed. The Environmental Crisis: The Ethical Dilemma.** Mancelona, MI: The AuSable Trails Institute of Environmental Studies, 1982. 375 pages.

A cross section of opinions and ideas emerging out of a Christian stewardship conference held at AuSable Trails Institute for Environmental Studies in Mancelona, Michigan. Illustrates the diversity of views among Christian ecologists while emphasizing the need for commitment and action in creating a morally sound environmental ethic. Contributions by Hans Schwarz, "Toward a Christian Stewardship of the Earth: Promise and Utopia" (pp. 21–38), Merald Westpahl; "Existentialism and Environmental Ethics" (pp. 77–90), Keith Yandell; "Fundamentals of Environmental Ethics: East and West" (pp. 91–107); and Thomas Compton, "Natural Resource Stewardship: The Earth Is the Lord's" (pp. 109–114). A good presentation of stewardship Christian views and their application to ecological practice.

247. **Stone, Christopher. Earth and Other Ethics: The Case for Moral Pluralism.** New York, NY: Harper & Row, 1987. 280 pages.

An expansion of the author's earlier and now classic, *Should Trees Have Standing?* (1974), this well-argued brief expands the question of "tree rights" to the entire biotic community. In doing so, Stone defends a moral pluralism, that, in contrast to ethical monism, adopts no singular ethical system for protecting the earth's biosphere.

In some circumstances, argues Stone, one might protect nature simply because of utilitarian concerns for clean drinking water; in others, because of a profound sense of religious or moral duty to "God's creation." More than half of the book is simply a technical defense of this position, which often leads Stone far astray from what appears to be the task at hand—the creation of an environmental ethic strong enough to save the planet from environmental destruction. Perhaps Stone is aware that the pluralistic platform he advocates has the innate potential for developing into a relativistic ethical system and therefore must go to pains to defend this "multiple-criterion position" (see chapter 17, "A Meta-ethical Unwinding," pp. 241–258).

On the question of rights of nonhuman animals, Stone creates a "hierarchy of sentience," in which higher animals receive a "higher" moral status than "lower" ones—nonhuman animals are placed on different, though not entirely separate, moral planes. In this view, nonhuman animals, because "they are different in morally salient ways," cannot be given the same valuational status as humans; i.e., they perform different life-enhancing functions and must be "graded" according to standards of moral utility (p. 218). Stone does not view nonhuman entities as *moral agents*, however, reserving this ethical distinction for persons only. A cogent and challenging argument for the adoption of multiple-use criterian in assessing our duties to the natural world. Notes.

248. **Stone, Christopher. Should Trees Have Standing?: Toward Legal Rights for Natural Objects.** Los Altos, CA: William Kaufmann, Inc., 1974. 102 pages.

A reprinted and highly controversial article which originally appeared in the University of Southern California Law Review. A professor of law, Stone proposes that trees, mountains, forests, rivers, beaches, in fact—all natural resources—have the same legal rights as humans. The writing is technical, the opening chapters constituting a philosophical, albeit persuasive, argument of mostly legal principles. Appendix. Foreword by Garrett Hardin.

249. **Storer, John. The Web of Life: A First Book of Ecology.** New York, NY: Devin-Adair, 1954. 144 pages.

A simple and direct statement on the interdependence of all life. Lucid, at times, poetic. Introduction by Fairfield Osborn.

250. **Taylor, Paul W. Respect for Nature: A Theory of Environmental Ethics.** Princeton, NJ: Princeton University Press, 1986. 329 pages.

According to the author, a professor of philosophy at Brooklyn College, "[e]nvironmental ethics is concerned with the moral relations that hold between humans and the natural world. The ethical principles governing those relations determine our duties, obligations, and responsibilities with regard to the Earth's natural environment and all the animals and plants that inhabit it" (p. 3). From that opening statement the author proceeds to methodically outline what he calls a "biocentric outlook on nature" (chapter 3, pp. 99–168), an environmental ethic that recognizes: (1) "all organisms are teleological centers," (2) "humans are members of the Earth's Community of Life in the same sense and on the same terms in which other living things are members of that Community," (3) "human species, along with all other species, are integral elements in a system of interdependence such that the survival of each living thing, as well as its chances of fairing well or poorly, is determined not only by the physical condition of its environment but also by its relations to other living things," (4) "humans are not inherently superior to other living things" (pp. 99–100).

After defending each of those principles in detail, Taylor proceeds to outline his own ethical system, a non-anthropocentric environmental ethic "that moral agents would be guided by if they were to accept the biocentric outlook and take the attitude of respect for nature" (p. 169). Interestingly, the author does not make claims to the moral rights of plant and animal life, arguing that the concept of moral rights is something that logically, and rationally, can be applied only to persons. *Respect for Nature* concludes with a qualifying chapter on "competing claims and priority principles," establishing the normative function of the author's ethical idea. A well-argued and comprehensive view of human/nature relations. Bibliography.

251. **Thomas, Keith. Man and the Natural World: A History of the Modern Sensibility.** New York, NY: Pantheon Books, 1983. 425 pages.

"Expanded version of the George Macaulay Trevelyan lectures delivered at the University of Cambridge in Lent term 1979" (Preface). A well-documented, historically rich volume, *Man and the Natural World* surveys the emergence of non-utilitarian attitudes toward nature, in England, from approximately 1500 to 1800. Drawing from a range of sources, the author documents the change from anthropocentric views of animals and plants to our present modern ones. Extensive notes; illustrations with list of sources.

252. **Thomas, Lewis. The Medusa and the Snail: More Notes of a Biology Watcher.** New York, NY: Viking Press, 1979. 146 pages.

A collection of short essays by the author of *The Lives of a Cell* (1974), Lewis Thomas addresses issues surrounding recent biological research and applies them to the unique complexity of the human condition. Topics are varied, and sometimes of little relevance to ecophilosophical issues. Nevertheless, insightful observations on the eternal questions of disease, life, and death in nature.

253. **Thompson, William Irvin. The Time Falling Bodies Take to Light.** New York, NY: St. Martin's Press, 1981. 280 pages.

In this synthesis of mythology, anthropology, psychology, and religion, meta-historian William Irvin Thompson raises fundamental questions about sexuality, consciousness, culture and nature. In Part Three, "Western Civilization and the Displacement of the Feminine," Thompson upholds feminine ways of knowing as being ecologically sensitive, saying they are more closely linked to nature's rhythms and bio-physical periodicities.

"[W]omen," says the author, "were the first observers of the basic periodicity of nature, the periodicity upon which all later scientific observations were made. Woman was the first to note a correspondence between an internal process she was going through and an external process in nature. She is the one who constructs a more holistic epistemology in which subject and object are in sympathetic resonance with one another. She is the holistic scientist who constructs a taxonomy for all the beneficial herbs and plants; she is the one who knows the secrets of the time of their flowering. The world view that separates the observer from the system he observes, that imagines that the universe can be split into mere subjectivity and real objectivity, is not of her doing" (p. 97). Notes. Gender and Culture. Ecofeminism.

254. **Thompson, William Irvin, ed. Gaia: A New Way of Knowing.** New York, NY: The Lindisfarne Press, 1988. 217 pages.

Gaia, the Greek goddess of Earth, is connected to ecophilosophy circles today by the hypothesis advanced in 1975 by James Lovelock and Lynn Margulis—the Gaia hypothesis. This hypothesis, which deals with the self-regulating effects of organic life on earth's atmosphere, also includes the perception of our planet as a single living entity. The Gaian metaphor has now been extended into the political sphere as William Irvin Thompson uses it in this anthology to critique the modern political practices of postindustrial nations. A Gaian politics, says Thompson, will create a new understanding of the interpenetration of all life, a new ecology of consciousness in which political practices arise out of an informed understanding of living systems (See chapter 9, pp. 167–214). Other notable selections by Gregory Bateson, James Lovelock, Lynn Margulis, John Todd, and Hazel Henderson.

255. **Thoreau, Henry David. The Selected Works of Thoreau.** Boston, MA: Houghton Mifflin, 1975. 851 pages.

A reprint of the original Cambridge Edition of the *Works of Thoreau*, edited by Henry Seidel Canby in 1937. Canby's selections were based on the twenty-one volume edition of *The Writings of Thoreau*, which were edited by Francis H. Allen and Bradford Torrey and published by the Houghton Mifflin publishing company in 1906 as the Walden Edition (long since regarded as the standard edition by Thoreau scholars). Contains Thoreau's most influential writings. Introduction by Walter Harding.

256. **Tichi, Cecelia. New World, New Earth: Environmental Reform in American Literature from the Puritans through Whitman.** New Haven, CT: Yale University Press, 1979. 290 pages.

An informed reassessment of the Puritan's role in shaping environmental attitudes in America. As the author notes in the preface, scholars and analysts alike have told us that the Puritans ignored the stewardly obligations intended in Scripture's authorization of dominion over the earth. The general belief is that the Puritans took dominion to mean, carte blanche, the promiscuous use of New World natural resources: its flora and fauna. This view, asserts the author, is for the most part inaccurate—a largely unchallenged assumption easily corrected by an acute historical study of Puritan religious beliefs and attitudes toward nature.

Tichi's own study provides a detailed, rigorously documented account of the various literary, religious, and environmental themes emerging out of the literature and historical period in question. She ultimately argues that the origins and temperament that would lead to land-reform, and the destruction of the New World environment, derives not from the book of Genesis but from the prophetic Book of Revelation. Married ideologically to the American spirit of manifest destiny, Puritan *millennialism* created the soil out of which an unchecked environmental reform could grow. Extensive notes provides a substantial bibliography.

257. Tichi, Cecelia. **Shifting Gears: Technology, Literature, Culture in Modernist America.**
Chapel Hill, NC: University of North Carolina Press, 1987. 310 pages.

During the early part of this century, the machine and its metaphor had a profound effect on American consciousness and culture, influencing perception, language, and social structure. In *Shifting Gears*, Tichi, a professor of English at Boston University, documents the emergence of the machine in American life from the 1890s to the 1920s. Offering a straight forward analysis of technology's impact on modern life, she argues that mechanical inventions, and the structures created by these devices, transformed our relationship not only to nature but to art as well, especially the literary arts. "The proliferation of machines and structures in American life between the 1890's and the 1920's began to make itself felt in popular and serious fictions," writes Tichi. "Novels of commercial and artistic intent showed a new consciousness of a world of 'trees, animals, engines'" (p. 18). With the emergence of the machine as the dominant metaphor, adds Tichi, the distance between nature and technological inventions was narrowed; one found it more and more difficult to write about the natural world without resorting to language borne of technological principles. A profound and creative work. Postscript.

258. **Tobias, Michael. After Eden: History, Ecology and Conscience.** San Diego, CA: Avant Books, 1985. 376 pages.

Following the thesis of ecophilosopher Paul Shepard, Tobias argues that the human race lost paradise on earth when it shifted from a hunting and gathering existence to one of agriculture and authoritarian pastoralism. The author weaves his own thesis by drawing on paleontology, anthropology, mythology, cultural history, literature, evolution, and ecology. Tobias suggests that Earth *is* paradise and that we should reorder human life accordingly. Selected bibliography.

259. **Tobias, Michael, ed. Deep Ecology.** San Diego, CA: Avant Books, 1985. 296 pages.

Published almost simultaneously, Tobias' anthology of deep ecology literature makes an excellent companion volume to Devall and Sessions' work by that same title. The text contains essays by some of the most noted ecophilosophers writing in the field: Arne Naess, Murray Bookchin, Gary Snyder, Paul Shepard, Garrett Hardin, and Roderick Nash, to name but six of the twenty-one authors represented in this work. Unlike the text of Devall and Sessions, the interdisciplinary thrust of the deep ecology literature is made immediately apparent by Tobias' more eclectic version of deep ecology. The essays range from Tobias' own "Humanity and Radical Will" (pp. 2–27), to Alan Grapard's "Nature and Culture in Japan" (pp. 240–255). There are also notable entries by Herman Daly, Dolores LaChapelle, and William Catton. Notes.

260. **Tokar, Brian. The Green Alternative: Creating an Ecological Future.** San Pedro, CA: R.& E. Miles, 1987. 174 pages.

A three-part analysis of Green principles and activities in North America, *The Green Alternative* provides a timely and introductory account of where the Green movement has been and where it is going. Gives detailed examples of how current grassroots activism, inspired by Green principles, combines ecological awareness with political responsibility and community organizing. Addresses also the issues of bioregionalism, the socio-economic roots of ecological degradation; the importance of creating a uniquely North American Green Party. Selected chapters include 3, "Ecology: The Art of Living on the Earth" (pp. 58–79); 4, "Social Justice and Responsibility" (pp.80–96); and 7, "How Can We Create a Green Future?" (pp.134–150). Annotated notes on sources.

261. **Trimble, Stephen. Words from the Land: Encounters with Natural History Writing.**

Salt Lake City, UT: Peregrine Smith Books,
1988. 303 pages.

"Contemporary natural history writers speak for the earth," begins
Stephen Trimble's introduction to this well-edited anthology. "They articulate our neglected connections with the rest of the living world in language
both passionate and thoughtful" (p. 2). What follows is a collection of previously published essays by philosophers, biologists, naturalists and jour-
nalists recognized for their natural history and/or related writings: John
McPhee, Annie Dillard, Edward Abbey, Gretel Ehrlich, Sue Hubbell, Barry
Lopez, and Wendell Berry are among the sixteen authors represented in this
volume.

Each selection is prefaced with a photograph and biographical sketch of
the author, giving further insight into the contributor's personal motivation
for writing about things natural. We find, for example, that some of the es-
sayists do not consider themselves "environmentalists"—they, like John Mc-
Phee, emphasize the more human elements of nature writing, claiming that
their work says as much about people as it does about the environment. The
entries in this volume, however, speak directly from experiences in "unpeopled" landscapes. We are given a variety of ecological terrains on which
to ponder the question of man, nature, and the value of uninhabited wilderness.

262. **Tuan, Yi-Fu. Topophilia: A Study of
Environmental Perception, Attitudes and
Values.** Englewood Cliffs, NJ: Prentice-Hall,
1974. 260 pages.

Mindscapes, landscapes, and ecological architecture. A humanistic geographer writes about environmental perception, our aesthetic interaction with
natural surroundings. Topophilia (literally, love of place) requires a certain
appreciation for the "geometry of natural space," argues Tuan. We participate
our environments as part of ourselves—dwell ecologically in those natural
places—only by creating structures that maintain the integrity of topo-
geographic domains. Humanistic Geography and Ecological Architecture.
Illustrations; map.

263. **Tuan, Yi-Fu. Segmented Worlds and Self:
Group Life and Individual Consciousness.**
Minneapolis, MN: University of Minnesota
Press, 1982. 222 pages.

In *Segmented Worlds and Self*, Tuan explores the human-environmental
landscapes, the psychological ambience of space, place, and perception.
Tuan recounts the many historical and cultural factors involved in shaping
our modern concepts of self and self-knowledge; and using evidence from

both Eastern and Western sources, criticizes the highly interiorized consciousness of the modern individual. In order to recapture the cohesive objectivity of persons in touch with their surroundings and communities, the author argues that "individuals" must interact more faithfully, more nonreflexively, with their environments. In chapter 6, "Ambience and Sight" (pp. 114-136), Tuan considers bringing back all the senses into the experiential milieu, arguing that modern society is too preoccupied with visual metaphors and single "visions." A serious and scholarly reflection on a possible ecological reconstruction of the fragmented modern individual. Notes.

264. **Tucker, William. Progress and Privilege: America and the Age of Environmentalism.** Garden City, NY: Anchor Press/Doubleday, 1982. 314 pages.

A rather tendentious and sometimes ill-informed critique of American environmentalism. The author argues that the environmental movement serves only the interests of the upper-middle class, and is used primarily to protect the status quo at the expense of less-privileged classes. This book is beneficial only in that it provides critical and necessary arguments against environmental elitism, or "ecology without a conscience."

265. **Vance, Mary. Human Ecology: Monographs Published in the 1980s.** Monticello, IL: Vance Bibliographies, 1986. 58 pages. (Public Administration Series, p. 21–73).

Vance Bibliographies has compiled a number of reference lists of works either directly or indirectly related to ecophilosophical pursuits. *Human Ecology: Monographs Published in the 1980s* provides 543 current titles on topics ranging from human ecology and environmental history, to human geography and environmental science. Selections are from American, European, and Asian publishing houses (including the Soviet Union), with an unusually good representation of Latin American texts. Other pertinent bibliographies in this series include: *Man's Influence on Nature: Monographs*; *Landscape and Nature Aesthetics: Monographs*; *The Negotiation of Environmental Conflicts: Techniques, Case Studies, and Analyses*; and *Social Ecology: Monographs*.

266. **Vanden Broeck, Goldian, ed. Less Is More: The Art of Voluntary Poverty.** San Francisco, CA: Harper & Row, 1978. 316 pages.

As in Duane Elgin's *Voluntary Simplicity* (1982), this anthology looks at ways in which the simple life can be both a virtuous and desirable one. Under headings like "In Praise of Poverty," "Eco-logic," and "Choosing the Image:

Life/Styles," the editor has arranged hundreds of quotations from both scholarly and religious texts. The juxtapositioning of the various aphorisims, maxims, and abridged quotations brings the thought of a number of important thinkers into the discussion—in ways one might not appreciate in other contexts. An excellent sourcebook for ecophilosophers. Preface by E.F. Schumacher.

267. **Vecsey, Christopher, and Venables, Robert W., eds. American Indian Environments: Ecological Issues in Native American History.** Syracuse, NY: University of Syracuse Press, 1980. 208 pages.

A series of essays that examine the philosophy and reality of Native American interaction with the environment. The studies discuss and analyze the relationship between Indians and nature in both historical and contemporary settings. Specific topics vary, ranging from environmental religion to the exploitation of energy resources on contemporary reservations.

268. **Walker, Stephen. Animal Thought.** London, England: Routledge & Kegan Paul, 1983. 437 pages.

A look at the mental life of non-human species, this book examines past and present theories of animal thought, perception and intelligence. Walker, a psychology professor at the University of London, Birkbeck, provides readers with a healthy balance of philosophical and scientific literature and his own personal insights. His critique of Descartes' view of human and animal nature is an informed one, although the reviewer noticed no overt references to Leonora Rosenfield's *From Beast-Machine to Man-Machine* (1968). Walker concludes that the mental life of animals, especially mammals, is on a very similar continuum with our own. An important contribution to the study of animal awareness, with peripheral relevance to animal rights theory and practice. Notes.

269. **Wallace, David Rains. Idle Weeds: The Life of a Sandstone Ridge.** San Francisco, CA: Sierra Club Books, 1980. 183 pages.

Acute observations of nature by a noted naturalist and author. The narrative concerns the flora and fauna of a sandstone ridge in eastern central Ohio. The book presents the author's views on broader philosophical issues and planetary concerns. Glossary of plants and animals mentioned in the text. Natural history, plant and animal ecology.

270. **Wallace, David Rains. The Klamath Knot: Explorations of Myth and Evolution.**

San Francisco, CA: Sierra Club Books, 1983. 149 pages.

The Klamaths, or more precisely, the Klamath Mountains of Oregon and northern California, are the setting for the author's natural history account of evolution and ecological change. One does not need to know the Klamoths, however, in order to appreciate the author's observant observations of them. An inspired and imaginative portrait of nature in motion, nature at rest; *The Klamath Knot* ties mystery to natural science, mythology to historical geology. Natural history.

271. **Watson, Lyall. Lifetide: The Biology of the Unconscious.** New York, NY: Simon and Schuster, 1979. 364 pages.

A roaming exegesis on the unconscious, the paranormal, evolution, the biological origins of life—the divergent and dynamic world around us. Watson, a respected scientist who has worked in a number of different fields, catalogs the "anomalies" of the life sciences in order to illustrate the symbiotic relationship between all living things.

272. **Watts, Alan. Man, Nature, and Woman.** New York, NY: Pantheon, 1958. 221 pages.

In this work, the author argues that Western man tries to control and subdue nature. Eastern ways of knowing (Taoism, Buddhism) are participatory and see nature as an organic whole in which man/woman is an interrelated part. New attitudes toward nature would recouple the bond between humans and nature, man and woman, humanity and God: "The rift between God and nature would vanish if we knew how to experience nature, because what keeps us apart is not a difference of substance but a split in the mind" (pp. 188–189).

273. **Watts, Alan. Tao: The Watercourse Way.** New York, NY: Pantheon, 1975. 134 pages.

The history and religious psychology of philosophical Taoism. Alan Watts, a major interpreter of Eastern thought to Western readers, links the principles of Taoism to ecocentric awareness and practice. Introduction by Al Chung Liang.

274. **Weizsacker, Carl Friedrich von. The Unity of Nature.** Trans. Francis Zucker. New York, NY: Farrar, Straus & Giroux, 1980. 406 pages.

A collection of previously published essays by the author, a well-known German physicist and professor of philosophy. The text, dealing primarily with the philosophy of science, introduces and extends upon such topics as quantum theory, information theory, the theory of language, cybernetics, and the Platonic theory of Forms. Perhaps too obtuse for the general reader, this book may be better suited for the academic specialists working in the philosophy of organic and/or inorganic science.

275. **Wenz, Peter. Environmental Justice.**
Albany, NY: State University of New York
Press, 1988. 384 pages (in press).

276. **Wilkinson, Loren. Earthkeeping: Christian Stewardship of Natural Resources.** Grand
Rapids, MI: William B. Eerdmans, 1980.
317 pages.

Earthkeeping is a creative presentation of essays, charts, and graphs calling for a proper stewardship of the earth's natural resources. The authors maintain that Christian beliefs and practices have influenced dominant attitudes toward nature, but disagree with Lynn White's thesis that Christianity is solely responsible for the present ecological crisis. Section II of the text (part A) provides four historical "views of nature," including those of the ancient Greeks, and ends with a survey entitled "The North American Experience" (pp. 135–143). A fundamental introductory text toward developing a distinctly Christian approach to taking responsibility for the ecology of the planet.

277. **Wilson, E. O. Biophilia.** Cambridge, MA:
Harvard University Press, 1984. 157 pages.

A personal statement, part autobiographical, part philosophical, by the Frank B. Baird Jr. Professor of Science at Harvard University. Fortunately, Wilson leaves behind many of his socio-biological arguments (see, for example, *On Human Nature*, 1978), emphasizing in this work the organic matrix linking humans to the diverse biotic community. As defined by Wilson, biophilia is "the innate tendency to focus at life and lifelike processes." *Biophilia*, the book, focuses nicely on living things and reads as a poetic testament to the author's appreciation for the natural world.

278. **Winner, Langdon. Autonomous Technology: Technics-out-of-Control as a Theme in Political Thought.** Cambridge, MA: MIT
Press, 1977. 386 pages.

A penetrating examination of the effects of technology on society and consciousness. The idea of autonomous technology—"the belief that somehow technology has gotten out of control and follows its own course, independent of human direction" (p. 13)—is an idea that Winner has borrowed from Jacques Ellul (whose work on technique is perhaps without equal). While retaining Ellul's critical posture, Winner extends his critique into several spheres, including politics, the domination of nature, and the institutional infrastructure. A good scholarly overview of the politics of technology and its primary role in determining political and social life. Extensive notes.

279. **Winner, Langdon. The Whale and the Reactor: A Search for Limits in an Age of High Technology.** Chicago, IL: The University of Chicago Press, 1986. 200 pages.

In the "age of simulation," the effects of technology on social and personal life are profound to say the least. Modern technology not only transforms human experience, it also creates the cultural conditions in which critiques of technology have little or no meaning in our daily lives. Our inability to effectively discuss the negative aspects of technology, or technological change, allows us to irresponsibly accept the technological "advance" as intrinsically beneficial and politically correct. In ten self-contained essays, the author, an associate professor of political science at the Rensselaer Polytechnic Institute, examines these and other issues related to a critical philosophy of technology. In chapter 7, "The State of Nature Revisited" (pp. 121–137), the author provides a brief but informed critical overview of contemporary nature philosophy and its leading proponents and concepts. Overall, an advanced and stimulating discussion on the philosophical, political, and social implications of technology. Notes.

280. **Woodhouse, Tom, ed. People and Planet.** Devon, England: Green Books, 1987. 220 pages.

A five-part collection of speeches by Alternative Nobel Prize recipients. The awards, which go to individuals who have worked on developing new approaches to problems in the areas of human rights, people's economics, ecological conservation, and appropriate technology, are given annnually by the Right Livelihood Foundation of Great Britian. Chapter 1, "The Rights of the Earth" (pp. 3–55), includes essays by Petra Kelly, Amory and Hunter Lovins, Duna Kor, and Wangari Maathai. Chapter 2, "People's Economics" (pp. 59–97), looks at the problems surrounding alternative economic development and includes essays by Leopold Kohr, Pat Mooney, and Leif Sandholt. Chapter 3, "The Cooperative Community" (pp. 101–128), discusses rural development in Third World countries; chapter 4, "Human Centered Technology" (pp. 133–165) defends, in the spirit of E.F. Schumacher, appropriate-scale technologies. Chapter 5, "The Rights of People" (pp. 169–220), concludes the volume with six entries, including Rajni Kothari's "Grassroots Development" (pp. 191–200) and Patrick van Rensburg's "Education for Social Change" (pp. 214–220).

281. **Worster, Donald, ed. American Environmentalism: The Formative Period, 1860–1915.** New York, NY: John Wiley and Sons, 1973. 233 pages.

Beginning with George Perkins Marsh's "Study of Nature" in 1860, Worster surveys 55 years of American environmentalism. The text is divided into four parts ("Man and Nature in an Age of Science," "The Conservation Movement," "Garden City and Suburb," and "The Biocentric Revolution") and uncovers the images of prominent American environmentalists, extracting selections from their most important work. Partial contents include: Lester Ward, "The Psychic Factors of Civilization" (pp. 39–53), Gifford Pinchot, "The Fight for Conservation" (pp. 84–95), Charles W. Eliot, "The Need of Conserving the Beauty and Freedom of Nature in Modern Life" (pp. 177–184), Nathaniel Shaler, "The Emergence of an Ecological Consciousness" (pp. 209–222). Part Four, "The Biocentric Revolution" should be of important interest to ecophilosophers. Suggested reading list.

282. **Worster, Donald. Nature's Economy: The Roots of Ecology.** San Francisco, CA: Sierra Club Books, 1977. 404 pages.

The author traces the history of ecology, beginning with its classical origins in the eighteenth century. Worster's historical study of the "economy of nature" places noticeable emphasis on the development of ecological thought as it has evolved in either a direct or indirect relationship to changing scientific and cultural attitudes. Worster examines, in detail, the work of Frederic Clemons, Aldo Leopold, Eugene Odum, and dozens of other ecologists, summarizing their various contributions to the study and evolution of ecological science.

In chapter 4, "Nature Looking into Nature" (pp. 77–97), Worster links ecological perceptions of nature to the romantic traditions of Goethe, Wordsworth, and Thoreau. According to Worster, the romantic tradition saw the world in its most alive and organic state. "Romanticism was fundamentally biocentric," proclaims the author. "This doctrine proposes that all nature is alive, and whatever is alive has a claim on man's moral affections. With the Romantics, a sense of antagonistic dualism gave way to a movement toward fusion, and anthropocentric indifference toward nature yielded to a love for the whole order of being and an acknowledgement of natural kinship" (p. 85). Glossary of terms. Extensive notes.

283. **Zweers, Wim, and Achterberg, W., eds. Environmental Crisis and Philosophy: Western Consciousness and Alienated**

Nature. Amsterdam, Holland: Ecological
Press, 1984. 212 pages.

A collection of ecophilosophical essays, in Danish, by seven Dutch philosophers. The first major publication of its kind in that country.

APPENDIX A

Periodicals, Journals, Newsletters

284. **Environmental Ethics**
Eugene Hargrove, Editor
Department of Philosophy
University of Georgia
Athens, Georgia 30602

An interdisciplinary journal, published quarterly, "dedicated to the philosophical aspects of environmental problems." One of the leading, if not the leading, environmental philosophy publication. Provides featured articles, discussion papers, and substantial book reviews. Annual cumulative index.

285. **Environmental Review**
William G. Robbins, Editor
Department of History
Oregon State University
Corvallis, OR 97331

Published by the American Society for Environmental History, *Environmental Review* is "an international quarterly journal that seeks understanding of human ecology through the perspectives of history and the humanities." A leading ecophilosophy journal. Feature articles and book reviews.

286. **The Ecologist**
Worthyvale Manor Farm
Camelford, Cornwall
England PL32 9TT

Published six times a year, *The Ecologist* "is one of the few journals still prepared to give its authors the space to consider, in-depth, the environmental and social issues facing the world today—and their philosophical implications." Recommended.

287. **Ecophilosophy**
George Sessions, Editor
Sierra College
Rockland, CA 95677–3397

The editor, a professor of philosophy and co-author of *Deep Ecology* (1985), provides a "state-of-the-art" newsletter and literature review of ecophilosophical texts. Contains information about all aspects of ecophilosophy. Available annually.

288. **The Trumpeter**
Alan Drengson, Editor
LightStar: P.O. Box 5853
Victoria, B.C., Canada V8R–6S8

"Voices from the Canadian Ecophilosophy Network." An excellent journal, published quarterly, that aims to provide a diversity of perspectives on the human-nature relationship and is "dedicated to [the] exploration of and contributions to a new ecological consciousness and sensibility." Contains current information on books, periodicals, organizations, and conferences.

289. **Not Man Apart**
1045 Sansome Street
San Francisco, CA 94111

The bimonthly publication of the Friends of the Earth. The authors tend to stress the use of alternative energy sources and focus primarily on issues related directly to FOE activities. Contains reviews, essays, news items, etc. Illustrated. 15 to 20 pages.

290. **Firmament**
NACCE Quarterly
309 Front Street
Traverse City, Michigan 49684

A quarterly devoted to expressing the ecological dimensions of Christianity and Christian thought. The journal is the product of The North American Conference on Christianity and Ecology, Inc., a nonprofit organization that has recently formed to "elucidate the ecological dimension inherent in Christianity, and to help churches, and organizations with their ecological work." Book reviews, book lists, and bibliographies. Calendar and announcements.

291. **The Eleventh Commandment Newsletter**
Vincent Rossi, Editor
P.O. Box 14727
San Francisco, CA 94114

A newsletter published by the Eleventh Commandment Fellowship, which believes that "the Earth is the Lord's and the fullness thereof; thou shalt not despoil the Earth nor destroy the life thereon." Articles, poetry, illustrations. Christian stewardship.

292. **The Deep Ecologist**
John Martin, Editor
10 Alamein Avenue

Warracknabeal, Victoria
Australia

Australia provides some of the most progressive ecophilosophy literature available. John Passmore, Peter Singer, Richard and Val Routley, Ariel Kay Salleh, Warwick Fox, et al., are all inhabitants of that vast, biologically diverse, continent. *The Deep Ecologist* is a newsletter published in Australia by John Martin and is dedicated to preserving a deep ecology perspective and practice. It publishes articles and materials on deep ecology, conferences, books, and all activities related to ecophilosophy.

293. **Alternatives**
Robert Gibson, Editor
Faculty of Environmental Studies
The University of Waterloo
Waterloo, Ontario
Canada N2L–3G1

An environmental quarterly that tries to "blend and balance the care and precision of scholarship with the timeliness and concern of citizen environmental activism." Features in-depth articles on land use, alternative energy strategies, pollution, and environmental health. Stressing the need for basic economic and political change, *Alternatives* has been called "Canada's leading environmental magazine." 40 to 60 pages. Book reviews.

294. **Ethics and Animals**
Harlan B. Miller, Editor
Department of Philosophy
Virginia Polytechnic Institute
Blacksburg, VA 24061

The quarterly journal of The Society for the Study of Ethics and Animals. Offers in-depth discussions on animal rights and welfare. Feature-length articles. Reviews.

295. **Inquiry**
Universitetsforlaget
P.O. Box 2959 Toyen
0608 Oslo 6, Norway

An interdisciplinary journal of philosophy and the social sciences, *Inquiry* was founded by ecophilosopher Arne Naess. While most of the articles generally have little or nothing to do with deep ecophilosophical issues, the journal frequently publishes such articles. See particularly Vol. 22, Nos. 1 and 2, (Summer 1979).

296. **Journal of Environmental Education**
4000 Albemarle St., N.W.
Washington, D.C. 20016

Published four times a year by the Helen Dwight Reid Educational Foundation, in association with the North American Association for Environmental Education. Assists educators at all levels in selecting appropriate information from the available environmental education curricula. Illustrations, references.

297. **Earth First! The Radical**
Environmental Journal
Dave Foreman, Editor
P.O. Box 5871
Tucson, Arizona 85703

Published eight times a year by the Earth First! organization, a "no-compromise environmental movement." Provides a variety of articles on "monkeywrenching" (eco-sabotage), ecophilosophy, and wilderness preservation. Book reviews, illustrations. 30 to 50 pages.

298. **Creation**
Matthew Fox, Editor
40 Santa Maria Way
Orinda, CA 94563

Published six times a year by Friends of Creation Spirituality, this journal celebrates the "sacredness of the earth and all its creatures." According to an editorial note, the goal of *Creation* is to "bring out the wisdom and mystery of the cosmos . . . as celebrated by today's sciences and the wisdom of Western mystics, primal peoples, and artists." Book reviews and other resources. Photographs.

299. **Harbinger: The Journal of Social Ecology**
P.O. Box 89
Plainfield, VT 05667

The journal of social ecology, *Harbinger* offers a substantial array of articles on both the practical and theoretical concerns of social ecology, ecological ethics, reconstructive anthropology, sustainable community design, and Green politics.

300. **The Whole Earth Review**
Kevin Kelley, Editor
27 Gate Five Road
Sausalito, CA 94965

A quarterly publication providing articles, book reviews, and features devoted to alternative lifestyles, ecological living, and personal empowerment. The March, 1985 issue (No. 45) offers considerable, albeit critical, coverage of environmental ethics and ecophilosophy.

301. Journal of Forest History
Harold K. Steen, Editor
Forest History Society
701 Vickers Avenue
Durham, NC 27701

Published quarterly by the Forest History Society in association with Duke University Press. The journal features article-length research on environmental history, as well as bibliographical and archival information, book reviews, and current news of the field. The "Biblioscope" section lists and annotates new books and articles on topics ranging from human ecology to wilderness preservation. Heavily illustrated with both photographs and artwork. Highly recommended.

302. Environmental History Newsletter
Bruce Piasecki, Editor
Clarkson University
Potsdam, NY 13676

The newsletter of the American Society for Environmental History. Short articles and reviews.

303. The Amicus Journal
Peter Borrelli, Editor
Clarkson University
Potsdam, NY 13676

Published quarterly by the National Defense Council. Feature-length articles and reports on environmental activities throughout North America. See particularly Peter Borrelli's essay in the Spring 1988 issue entitled, "The Ecophilosophers" (Vol. 10, No. 2, pp. 30–39.) Book reviews, poetry, letters. Well illustrated. Recommended.

304. The Newsletter for the International Network for Religion and Animals
P.O. Box 33061
Washington, D.C. 20033–0061

Provides information and other materials related to religious appreciation and respect for animals as well as networking information for animal rights activists.

305. **Pan Ecology**
Marsh Institute
P.O. Box 1
Viola, Idaho 83872–0001

An irregular journal of nature and human nature published by the Marshfield Institute of Idaho. Recent articles on ecosophy, sustainable land-use, and environmental ethics. Nicely illustrated.

306. **Environmental Action**
1525 New Hampshire Ave., N.W.
Washington, D.C. 20036

Published bimonthly by Environmental Action, Inc., a national political lobbying and education organization devoted to environmental protection. Book reviews and feature-length articles on a variety of topics related to environmental hazards and applied ecological activities.

307. **Resurgence**
Satish Kumar, Editor
Worthyvale Manoe Farm
Camelford, Cornwall
England PL32 9TT

A bi-monthly British magazine featuring articles, book reviews, and poetry on eco-political themes. Recent issues have included articles by Arne Naess, Jonathon Porritt, and Kirpatrick Sale. International in scope, this publication has offerings for readers on both sides of the Atlantic.

308. **The Egg: A Journal of Eco-Justice**
William Gibson, Editor
Anabel Hall
Cornell University
Ithaca, New York 14853

"Quarterly of the Eco-Justice Project and Network Center for Religion, Ethics and Social Policy." Contains well-edited essays on the relationship of ecology to social responsibility, economic development, and ethics. Reviews.

309. **Earth Island Journal**
Gar Smith, Editor
300 Broadway, Suite 28
San Francisco, CA 94133

An international environmental news magazine published by the Earth Island Institute. Features local news stories from around the globe. Reviews, letters, photography. 40–50 pages.

310. The Nature Conservancy News
1800 North Kent Street
Arlington, VA 22209

The official newsletter of The Nature Conservancy, containing articles on its current agenda, the status of North American wilderness areas, and general information. Well illustrated.

311. Sierra: The Sierra Club Bulletin
c/o The Sierra Club
730 Polk Street
San Francisco, CA 94109

The official bulletin of the Sierra Club. Publishes articles, news items, reports, and reviews. Considers impact on the environment of political and social issues, as well as providing information on camping, hiking, etc. Includes index in November/December issue. Magazine format with photography, illustrations, and advertising. Bimonthly.

312. Utne Reader
Eric Utne, Editor
P.O. Box 1974
Marion, Ohio 43305

"The best of the alternative press"—a bimonthly digest of articles and magazine reviews from alternative sources. Frequently contains articles related directly to ecophilosophical concerns. Recent issues have discussed bioregionalism, Green politics, deep ecology, environmental ethics, and alternative agriculture.

313. EcoSpirit
Donald St. John, Editor
Moravian College
Bethlehem, PA 18018

A small, independent publication featuring articles on ecophilosophy. Includes poetry and book reviews.

314. Minding the Earth
Joseph Meeker, Editor
Route 2, Box 256–A
Vashon Island, WA 98070

A occasional periodical produced by Joseph Meeker, the author of *The Comedy of Survival* (1974). Provides articles on a variety of ecological topics and issues.

315. **Raise the Stakes**
 Planet Drum Foundation
 Box 31251
 San Francisco, CA 94131

 Published bi-annually by the Planet Drum Foundation, an organization devoted to developing and communicating the concept of bioregionalism. Contains information about local bioregional activities and happenings, feature-length articles, reviews, and maps. Includes networking information.

316. **New Options**
 Mark Satin, Editor
 P.O. Box 19324
 Washington, DC 20036

 A small but informative newsletter summarizing political events, conferences, and other happenings related to ecological awareness. Timely letters and book reviews.

APPENDIX B

Learning Centers, Professional Organizations

317. Way of the Mountain Center
P.O. Box 542
Silverton, Colorado 81433

A clearinghouse and learning center for earth bonding rituals, ecological awareness, and ecophilosophy.

318. Institute for Social Ecology
P.O. Box 89
Plainfield, Vermont 05667

"Social ecology integrates the study of human and natural ecosystems through understanding the interrelationships of culture and nature. It advances a critical, holistic worldview and suggests that a creative human-enterprise can construct an alternative future, reharmonizing people's relationship to the natural world by reharmonizing their relationship with each other." This interdisciplinary approach involves the institute in studies concerning the natural sciences, feminism, anthropology, and philosophy, providing a coherent critique of current anti-ecological trends. Founded by Murray Bookchin and Dan Chodorkoff, the institute has been at the forefront of Green politics in the U.S., shaping the agendas of many Green groups across North America.

319. The Elmwood Institute
P.O. Box 5805
Berkeley, CA 94705

The Elmwood Institute was founded to nurture new ecological visions of reality based on awareness of the fundamental interdependence of all phenomena and of the embeddedness of individuals and societies in the cyclical processes of nature. Founding members include Fritjof Capra, Hazel Henderson, Ernest Callenbach, Charlene Spretnak, and Robert Livingston.

320. The Institute for Earth Education
Box 288
Warrenville, IL 60555

An Environmental Learning Center dedicated to helping "people live harmoniously and joyously with the natural world."

321. Defenders of Wildlife
1244 Nineteenth Street, N.W.

Washington, D.C. 20036

A national nonprofit educational organization and lobbying group, dedicated to the preservation of all forms of wildlife. Promotes, through education and research, the protection and humane treatment of mammals, birds, fish, and other wildlife. Publication: *Defenders*.

322. **The Nature Conservancy**
Suite 800
1800 North Kent Street
Arlington, VA 22209

A nonprofit membership corporation dedicated to the preservation of natural areas for present and future generations. Works closely with colleges, universities, public and private conservation organizations to acquire lands for scientific and educational purposes. Founded: 1946.

323. **Sierra Club**
530 Bush Street
San Francisco, CA 94108

Founded in 1892 by John Muir, the Sierra Club aims "to protect and conserve the natural resources of the Sierra Nevada, the United States, and the world; to undertake and publish scientific and educational studies concerning all aspects of man's environment and the natural ecosystems of the world; and to educate the people of the United States and the world of the need to preserve and restore the quality of that environment and the integrity of these ecosystems."

324. **World Wildlife Fund**
1601 Connecticut Avenue, N.W.
Suite 80
Washington, DC 20009

The largest private international conservation organization. The WWF initiates and supports programs directed at saving threatened and endangered wildlife and habits. Is also involved in scientific ecological research based predominantly upon the IUCN (International Union for Conservation of Nature and Natural Resources) World Conservation Strategy.

325. **Foundation on Emerging Technologies**
1130 17th Street, N.W.
Suite 630
Washington, DC 20036

The Foundation on Emerging Technologies is a non-profit organization actively involved in analyzing the environmental, ethical and philosophical implications of certain technological and social developments. The philosophy of the foundation is one that has become increasingly popular among the ecophilosophical constituency—and in accordance to this philosophy, ecological solutions to current economic and social problems are promoted by the foundation. The public is alerted to the potentially dangerous aspects of existing technologies and subsequently shown how these technologies are sometimes "mindlessly" propagated by the corporate and political elite. In short, the foundation serves the public as an informant through its books, litigation, and articles, offering alternative and often small-scale solutions to social problems.

326. Fauna Preservation Society
c/o Zoological Society of London
Regents' Park, London
England NW1 4RY

"To conserve wildlife throughout the world." A 4,000-member organization founded in 1903.

327. Friends of the Earth
124 Spear Street
San Francisco, CA 94105

"Committed to the preservation, restoration, and rational use of the earth's resources," Friends of the Earth is a citizen-based environmental organization working at both international and grassroots levels. The organization appears most effective in an advocacy role, where it actively educates the public to the environmental risks associated with toxic wastes, acid rain, nuclear power, and synthetic fuels.

328. The Humane Society of the United States
2100 L Street, N.W.
Washington, DC 20037

A national agency deeply committed to the prevention of cruelty to animals. HSUS major goals include reducing the overbreeding of cats and dogs; opposing sports hunting and trapping; educating people to respect all living things; correcting inhumane conditions in zoos and other exhibitions; ending cruelty in biomedical research and testing; monitoring federal laws to protect animals. Incorporated: November 1954.

329. The John Muir Institute
743 Wilson Street
Napa, CA 94558

A nonprofit membership organization, the John Muir Institute "seeks scientific information to expand knowledge about natural systems and the role of people in those systems. It seeks new policy approaches to improve the ways in which society manages, uses, and protects natural resources.... The Institute is interested as much in the social, economic, and institutional aspects of environmental problems as it is in the technical and physical aspects."

330. **Eco-Philosophy Centre**
1002 Granger
Ann Arbor, MI 48104

An ecophilosophy learning center which also publishes occasional booklets, monographs, and articles on ecophilosophy and related issues. Founded by Henryk Skolimowski.

331. **Forest History Society, Inc.**
701 Vickers Avenue
Durham, North Carolina 27701

A clearinghouse for information concerning "the utilization, management, and appreciation of our forest resources." Provides an array of consulting and referral services to all who use the field. The Society also sponsors research and publication activities, disseminating research findings through the publication of reference works, archival guides, and other sources. Established in 1955 as a nonprofit educational institution.

332. **Wilderness Psychology Group**
Department of Psychology
University of New Hampshire
Durham, NH 03824

An ad hoc group of students and professors concerned with the psychological effects of wilderness on human experience. Sponsors an annual conference on wilderness psychology.

333. **Schumacher Society**
Ford House. Hartland
Bideford, Devon
England EX39 6EE

The Schumacher Society, formed in 1977, is dedicated to promoting appropriate use technologies for developed, and developing countries. E.F. Schumacher, himself a visionary of human-scale economic systems, has provided inspiration for many contemporary ecophilosophers in works such as *Small Is Beautiful* and *A Guide for the Perplexed*. The society sponsors a series of lectures and events, involving many eminent thinkers and activists in the ecology movement. The society also has branches in West Germany and North America. American address: Box 76A, RD3, Great Barrington, Massachusetts, 01230.

334. Planet Drum Foundation
Box 31251
San Francisco, CA 94131

Founded in 1974 by Peter Berg, the Planet Drum Foundation actively promotes the concept of bioregionalism, an ecological idea envisioning a world based not on arbitrary political boarders, but on natural geographic regions defined by particular flora, fauna, landforms, and watersheds. The foundation has produced a number of educational materials to help facilitate this process, including books, newsletters, a directory, and maps.

INDEX

Bold numbers refer directly to entries authored or edited by the individuals or institutions listed. Items appearing in the foreward and introduction are indexed by page number; others are indexed using entry numbers.

Photo by Kim Tibbals

Donald Edward Davis holds master's degrees in both Social Ecology (Goddard College) and Psychology (West Georgia College). He has written a number of articles and reviews on environmental themes in such journals as the *Utne Reader*, *Environmental Ethics*, and *The Trumpeter*. Mr. Davis has, in addition, been a research assistant and consultant to the Foundation on Economic Trends in Washington, D.C., collaborating with Jeremy Rifkin on the recently published book *Time Wars: The Primary Conflict in Human History*. The author, having a deep appreciation for rural lifestyles and folk culture, works with a number of regional environmental groups in the Southeastern United States.